In Search of Lost Time - abridged

Zachary Whist

ISBN: 9798866888221

There must be some place along the route, a halfway house in time where the runners may pause and ask themselves why they run, what is the prize and is it the prize they really want? What became of Beauty, where went Love? There must be havens where they may be at least remembered.

Dawn Powell, The Wicked Pavilion

1 - SWANN'S WAY

For a long time I went to bed early. Sometimes, the candle barely out, my eyes closed so quickly that I did not have time to tell myself: "I'm falling asleep". Half an hour later the thought that it was time to look for sleep would awaken me; I would make as if to put away the book which I imagined was still in my hands, and to blow out the light. I had gone on thinking, while I was asleep, about what I had just been reading, but these thoughts had taken a peculiar turn; it seemed to me that I myself was the subject of my book; a church, a quarter, the rivalry between Francois I and Charles V. This impression would persist for some moments after I awoke; it lay like scales upon my eyes and prevented them from registering that the candle was no longer burning. Then it would begin to seem unintelligible, as the thoughts of a previous existence must after reincarnation; the subject of my book would separate itself from me, and at the same time my sight would return and I would be astonished to find myself in a state of darkness, pleasant and restful enough for my eyes but even more, perhaps, for my mind.

I would ask myself what time it could be; I could hear the whistling of trains which, now nearer and now further off; punctuating the distance like the note of a bird in a forest, showed me in perspective the deserted countryside through which a traveler is hurrying towards the nearby station. The path he is taking will be engraved in his memory by the strange surroundings, by the conversation he has had and the farewells exchanged beneath an unfamiliar lamp, and by the happy prospect of being home again.

I would fall asleep again, and thereafter would reawaken for short snatches only, just long enough to hear the regular creaking of the wainscot, or to open my eyes to stare at the shifting kaleidoscope of darkness, to savour, in a glimmer of consciousness, the sleep which lay heavy upon the furniture, the room, that whole of which I formed no more than a part and whose insensibility I should soon return to share. While sleeping I had drifted back to an earlier stage in my life, and had come under the thrall of one of my childish terrors, such as that of my great uncle pulling my curls, and as a measure of precaution I would bury the whole of my head in the pillow before returning to the world of dreams.

Sometimes, too, as Eve was created from a rib of Adam, a woman would be born during my sleep from some misplacing of my thigh. Conceived from the pleasure I was on the point of enjoying, she it was, I imagined, who offered me that pleasure. My body, conscious that its own warmth was permeating hers, would strive to become one with her, and I would awake. The rest of humanity seemed remote in comparison with this woman whose company I had left but a moment ago; my cheek was still warm from her kiss. If, as sometimes would happen, she had the features of some woman whom I had known in waking hours, I would abandon myself altogether to this end; to find her again, like people who set out on a journey to see with their eyes some city of their desire. And then, gradually, the memory of her would fade away; I had forgotten the girl of my dream.

When a man is asleep, he has in a circle round him the chain of the hours, the sequence of the years, the order of the heavenly bodies. Instinctively he consults them when he awakes, and in an instant reads off his own position on the earth's surface and the time that has elapsed during his slumbers; but this ordered procession is apt to grow confused, and to break its ranks. Suppose that he dozes off in some abnormal position, sitting in an armchair, for instance, after dinner. Then the world will go hurtling out of orbit, the magic chair will carry him at full speed through time and space, and when he opens his eyes again he will imagine that he went to sleep months earlier in another place. But for me it was enough if, in my own bed, my sleep was so heavy as completely to relax my consciousness; for then I lost all sense of the place in which I had gone to sleep, and when I awoke in the middle of the night, not knowing where I was, I could not even be sure at first who I was; I had only the most rudimentary sense of existence, such as may lurk and flicker in the depths of an animal. But then the memory

– not yet of the place in which I was, but of various other places where I had lived and might now be – would come like a rope let down from heaven to draw me out of the abyss of not-being, from which I could never have escaped myself.

 Perhaps the immobility of the things that surround us is forced upon them by our conviction they are themselves and not anything else. For it always happened that when I awoke like this, and my mind struggled in an unsuccessful attempt to discover where I was, everything revolved around me through the darkness: things, places, years. And even before my brain, hesitating at the threshold of times and shapes, had reassembled the circumstances sufficiently to identify the room, it would recall from each room the style of the bed, the position of the doors, the angle at which light came in at the windows, what I had had in my mind when I went to sleep there.

 Then the memory of a new position would spring up, and the wall would slide away in another direction; I was in my room in the country; good heavens, I must have overslept in the little nap which I always take when I come in from my walk with Mme de Saint-Loup. For many years have now elapsed since the Combray days when, coming in from the longest and latest walks, I would still be in time to see the reflection of the sunset glowing in the panes of my bedroom window. It is a very different kind of life one leads at Tansonville, at Mme de Saint Loup's, and a different kind of pleasure I derive from taking walks only in the evenings, from visiting by moonlight the roads on which I used to play as a child in the sunshine. As for the bedroom in which I must have fallen asleep instead of dressing for dinner, I can see it from the distance as we return from our walk, with its lamp shining through the window.

These shifting and confused gusts of memory never lasted for more than a few seconds, but I had seen first one and then another of the rooms in which I had slept during my life, and in the end I would revisit them all in the long course of my waking dream; rooms in winter, where on going to bed I would bury my head in a nest; rooms where, in freezing weather, I would enjoy the satisfaction of being shut in from the outer world and where I would sleep wrapped up in a great cloak of snug and smoky air shot with the glow of logs breaking out in flame, a cave of warmth dug out of the heart of the room itself – or rooms in summer, where I would delight to feel myself a part of the warm night, where the moonlight striking upon the half-opened shutters would throw down to the foot of my bed its enchanted ladder, where I would fall asleep like a titmouse at the tip of a sunbeam.

As a rule I did not attempt to go to sleep again at once, but used to spend the greater part of the night recalling our life in the old days at Combray with my great-aunt, at Balbec, Paris, Doncieres, Venice, and the rest; remembering again all the places and people I had known, what I had actually seen of them, and what others had told me.

2

At Combray, as every afternoon ended, my bedroom became the fixed point on which my anxious thoughts were centered. Someone had the happy idea of giving me, to distract me when I seemed wretched, a magic lantern, which used to be set on top of my lamp and, after the fashion of the glass painters of Gothic days, it substituted for my walls a supernatural phenomena of many colours, in which legends were depicted as on a shifting and transitory window. But my sorrows were only increased because this change was enough to destroy the familiar impression I had of my room. Now I no longer recognized it and felt uneasy in it, as in a place where I had just arrived by train for the first time.

Riding at a jerky trot, Golo issued from the little triangular forest which softened with dark green the slope of a hill, and advanced fitfully towards the castle of poor Genevieve de Brabant. In front of it stretched a moor on which Genevieve stood dreaming, wearing a blue girdle. Golo stopped for a moment and listened sadly to the accompanying patter read aloud by my great-aunt, which he seemed to understand, then he rode away at the same jerky trot. If the lantern were moved I could still distinguish Golo's horse advancing across the curtains, welling out with their curves and diving into their folds. The body of Golo himself overcame every obstacle by absorbing it into himself: even the doorknob - on which, adapting themselves at once, his red cloak or his pale face floated invincibly - would never betray the least concern.

After dinner, alas, I was soon obliged to leave Mamma, who stayed talking with the others, in the garden if it was fine, or in the little parlour where everyone took shelter when it was wet. Everyone except my grandmother, who held that "It's a pity to shut oneself indoors in the country" and used to have endless arguments with my father on the very wettest days, because he would send me up to my room with a book instead of letting me stay out of doors. "that is not the way to make him strong and active" she would say sadly "especially this little man, who needs all the strength and will-power that he can get"

Alas! I did not realise that my own lack of willpower, my delicate health, and the consequent uncertainty as to my future weighed heavily on my grandmother's mind, afternoon and evening, during which we used to see her handsome face passing to and fro, half raised towards the sky, while some sad reflection invariably left the drying traces of an involuntary tear.

My sole consolation when I went upstairs for the night was that Mamma would come in and kiss me after I was in bed. But this good night lasted for so short a time, she went down again so soon, that the moment in which I heard her climb the stairs, and then caught the sound of her garden dress rustling along the corridor, was for me a moment of the utmost pain; for it heralded the moment which was to follow it, when she would have left me and gone downstairs again. So much so that I reached the point of hoping this good night which I loved so much would come as late as possible, so to prolong the time of respite during which Mamma would not yet have appeared. Sometimes when, after kissing me, she opened the door to go, I longed to call her back, but I knew then she would at once look displeased, for the concession which she made in coming up to give me this kiss of peace always annoyed my father, who thought such rituals absurd, and she would have liked to induce me to outgrow the need of having her there at all, let alone get into the habit of asking her for an additional kiss when she was already crossing the threshold. And to see her displeased destroyed all the calm she had brought me a moment before.

But those evenings on which Mamma stayed so short a time in my room were sweet indeed compared to those on which we had people to dinner, and therefore she did not come at all. "People" were usually limited to M. Swann who, apart from a few passing strangers, was almost the only person who ever came to the house at Combray, sometimes to dinner (but less frequently since his marriage, as my family did not care to receive his wife) and sometimes after dinner, uninvited.   On those evenings when, as we sat in front of the house round the iron table beneath the big chestnut-tree, we heard from the far end of the garden the double tinkle, timid, oval, golden, of the visitor's bell, everyone would at once exclaim "A visitor! Who in the world can it be?" but they knew quite well that it could only be M. Swann. And then my grandmother, always happy to find an excuse for an additional turn in the garden, would be sent out to reconnoiter, and would take the opportunity to remove, as she passed, the stakes of a rose tree or two so as to make the roses look a little more natural, as a mother might run her hand through her boy's hair after the barber has smoothed it, to make it look more wavy.

We would all wait there in suspense for the report which my grandmother would bring back from the enemy lines, as though there might be a large number of possible assailants, and then my grandfather would say "I recognise Swann's voice". Although a far younger man, M Swann was very attached to my grandfather, who had been a friend of Swann's father, an excellent but eccentric man the current of whose thoughts would often be diverted by the most trifling thing. Several times in the course of a year I would hear my grandfather tell the story of the behaviour of M Swann the elder upon the death of his wife, by whose bedside he had watched day and night. My grandfather managed to entice him for a moment, weeping profusely, out of the death chamber, so that he should not be present when the body was laid in its coffin. They took a turn or two in the park, where there was a little sunshine. Suddenly M Swann seized my grandfather and cried "Ah my dear old friend, how fortunate we are to be walking here together on such a charming day! Don't you see how pretty they are, all these trees, my hawthorns, and my new pond, on which you have never congratulated me? You look as solemn as the grave. Don't you feel this little breeze? Ah! Whatever you may say, it's good to be alive all the same, my dear Amedee!" And then, abruptly, the memory of his dead wife returned to him. He never got over the loss of his wife, but used to say to my grandfather, during the years he survived her, "It's a funny thing; I very often think of my poor wife, but I cannot think of her for long at a time" "Often, but a little at a time, like poor old Swann" became one of my grandfather's favourite sayings, which he would apply to all manner of things.

For many years, during the course of which M Swann the younger came often to see them at Combray, my great aunt and my grandparents never suspected that they were harboring – with the complete innocence of a family of respectable innkeepers who have in their midst some celebrated highwayman without knowing it – one of the most distinguished members of the Jockey Club, a particular friend of the Comte de Paris and of the Prince of Wales, and one of the men most sought after in the aristocratic world of the Faubourg Saint-Germain.

Had it been absolutely essential to apply to Swann a social coefficient, as distinct from all the other sons of stockbrokers, his would have been rather lower because, being very simple in his habits, and having always had a "craze" for antiques and pictures, he now lived and amassed his collections in an old house which my grandmother longed to visit but which was situated on the Quai d'Orleans, a neighbourhood which my great-aunt thought most degrading. "Are you really a connoisseur at least?" she would say to him "I ask for your own sake, as you are likely to have fakes palmed off on you by the dealers" for she did not, in fact, endow him with any critical faculty, and had no great opinion of the intelligence of a man who would avoid serious topics and showed a dull preciseness, not only when he gave us kitchen recipes, going into the most minute details, but even when my grandmother's sisters were talking to him about art. When challenged by them to give an opinion, or to express his admiration for some picture, he would remain almost disobligingly silent, and would then make amends by furnishing (if he could) some fact or other about the gallery in which the picture was hung, or the date at which it had been painted. But as a rule he would content himself with trying to amuse us by telling us about his latest adventure with someone whom we ourselves knew, such as the Combray chemist, or our coachman. These stories certainly used to make my great-aunt laugh, but she could never decide whether this was on account of the absurd role which Swann invariably gave himself therein, or of the wit that he showed in telling them; "I must say you really are a regular character, M. Swann!"

But if anyone had suggested to my great-aunt that this Swann had another almost secret existence; that when he left our house in Paris, saying that he must go home to bed, he would no sooner have turned the corner than he would be off to some salon on whose like no stockbroker had ever set eyes – that would have seemed to my aunt as extraordinary as having had to dinner Ali Baba who, as soon as he finds himself alone and unobserved, will make his way into the cave, resplendent with unsuspected treasures.

One day when he had come to see us after dinner in Paris, apologising for being in evening clothes, Francoise told us after he had left that she had got it from his coachman that he had been dining "with a princess". "A nice sort of princess" retorted my aunt, shrugging her shoulders without raising her eyes from her knitting, serenely sarcastic.

 Altogether my great-aunt treated him with scant ceremony. Since she was of the opinion that he ought to feel flattered by our invitations, she thought it only proper that he should never come to see us without a basket of peaches or raspberries from his garden, and that from each of his visits to Italy he should bring back some photographs of old masters for me.

It seemed quite natural, therefore, to send for him whenever a recipe for some special sauce or for a pineapple salad was needed for one of our dinner parties, to which he himself would not be invited, being regarded as insufficiently important. If the conversation turned upon the princes of the House of France, "gentlemen you and I will never know, will we, and don't want to" my great-aunt would say tartly to Swann, who had, perhaps, a letter from Twickenham in his pocket; she would make him push the piano into place and turn over the music on evenings when my grandmother's sister sang, manipulating this person who was elsewhere so sought after.   Doubtless the Swann who was a familiar figure in all the clubs differed hugely from the Swann created by my great-aunt when, in our little garden at Combray, the obscure and shadowy figure emerged, with my grandmother in his wake, from the dark background. But then, even in the most insignificant details of our daily life, none of us can be said to constitute a material whole which is identical for everyone; our social personality is a creation of the thoughts of other people. Even the simple act which we describe as "seeing someone we know" is to some extent an intellectual process. We pack the physical outline of the person we see with all the notions we have formed about him, and in the total picture of him in our minds those notions have the principal place. Each time we see the face or hear the voice it is these notions we recognize and to which we listen. And so, no doubt, from the Swann they had constructed for themselves my family had left out details of his life, but they had also put into this face a memory of idle hours spent together after our weekly dinners, round the card-table or in the garden, during our companionable country life. Our friend's envelope had been so well lined that their own special Swann had become to my family a complete and living creature; so that even now I have the feeling of leaving someone I know for another person when, going back in memory, I pass from the Swann whom I knew later and more intimately to this early Swann – this early Swann in whom I can distinguish the charming mistakes of my youth – this Swann abounding in leisure, fragrant with the scent of the great chestnut tree, of baskets of raspberries and a sprig of tarragon.

This view of Swann's social position which prevailed in my family seemed to be confirmed later on by his marriage with a woman of the worst type, almost a prostitute, whom, to do him justice, he never attempted to introduce to us – for he continued to come to our house alone, but from whom they felt they could establish - on the assumption he had found her there – the circle in which he ordinarily moved.

Their interest grew, however, when, the day before Swann was to dine with us, and when he had made them a special present of a case of Asti, my great-aunt, who had in her hand a copy of the Figaro in which, to the name of a picture in a exhibition were added the words "from the collection of M Charles Swann" asked: "Did you see that Swann is mentioned in the Figaro?"

"But I've always told you" said my grandmother "that he had a great deal of taste". My grandmother's sisters having expressed a desire to mention to Swann this reference to him in the Figaro, my great-aunt dissuaded them. Whenever she saw in others an advantage, however trivial, which she herself lacked, she would persuade herself that it was no advantage at all, but a drawback, and would pity so as not to have to envy them. "I don't think that would please him at all; I know very well that I should hate to see my name printed like that, as large as life, in the paper, and I shouldn't feel at all flattered if anyone spoke to me about it."

As for my mother, her only thought was of trying to induce my father to speak to Swann, not about his wife but about his daughter, whom he worshipped, and for whose sake it was understood that he had ultimately made his unfortunate marriage. But the only one of us in whom the prospect of Swann's arrival gave rise to an unhappy foreboding was myself. This was because on evenings when there were visitors, or just M Swann, in the house, Mamma did not come up to my room. I dined before the others, and afterwards came and sat at table until eight o'clock, when it was understood that I must go upstairs. That frail and precious kiss which Mamma used normally to bestow on me when I was in bed and just going to sleep had to be transported from the dining room to my bedroom where I must keep it inviolate all the time that it took me to undress, without letting its sweet charm be broken.

And so it was that, for a long time afterwards, when I lay awake at night and revived old memories Combray, I saw no more of it than this sort of luminous panel, sharply defined against a vague and shadowy background, like the panels which the glow of a Bengal light or a searchlight beam will cut out and illuminate in a building plunged in darkness; broad enough at its base, the little parlour, the dining room, the opening of the dark path from which M Swann, the unwitting author of my sufferings, would emerge, the hall through which I would journey to the first step of that staircase, so painful to climb, which constituted, all by itself, the slender cone of this irregular pyramid and, at the summit, my bedroom, with the little passage through whose glazed door Mamma would enter; as though all Combray had consisted of but two floors joined by a slender staircase, and as though there had been no time there but seven o'clock at night. I must own that I could have assured any questioner that Combray did include other scenes and did exist at other hours than these. But since the facts which I should then have recalled would have been prompted only by voluntary memory, the memory of the intellect, and since the pictures which that kind of memory shows us preserve nothing of the past itself, I should never have had any wish. To me it was in reality all dead.

Permanently dead? Very possibly. There is a large element of chance in these matters, and a second chance occurrence - that of our own death - often prevents us from awaiting the favours of the first.

I feel there is much to be said for the Celtic belief that the souls of those whom we have lost are held captive in some inferior being, in an animal, in a plant, in some inanimate object, and thus effectively lost to us until the day (which to many never comes) when we happen to pass by the tree or to obtain possession of the object which forms their prison. Then they start and tremble, they call us by our name, and as soon as we recognize them the spell is broken. Delivered by us, they have overcome death and return to share our life. And so it is with our own past. It is a labour in vain to attempt to recapture it: all the efforts of our intellect prove futile. The past is hidden somewhere beyond the reach, in some material object. And it depends on chance whether or not we come upon this object before we ourselves must die.

3

Many years had elapsed during which nothing of Combray, except what lay in the theatre and the drama of my going to bed there, had any existence for me, when one day in winter, on my return home, my mother, seeing that I was cold, offered me some tea, a thing I did not oridinarily take. I declined at first, and then, for no particular reason, changed my mind. She sent for one of those squat, plump little cakes called petites madeleines, which look as thought they had been moulded in the fluted valve of a scallop shell. And soon, mechanically, dispirited after a dreary day with the prospect of a depressing morrow, I raised to my lips a spoonful of the tea in which I had soaked a morsel of the cake. No sooner had the warm liquid mixed with the crumbs touched my palate than a shiver ran through me and I stopped, intent upon the extraordinary thing that was happening to me. An exquisite pleasure had invaded my senses, something isolated, detached, with no suggestion of origin. And at once this new sensation had the effect, which love has, of filling me with a precious essence, or rather this essence was not in me, it *was* me. I had ceased to feel mediocre, contingent, mortal. Whence could it have come to me, this all-powerful joy? I sensed that it was connected with the taste of the tea and the cake, but that it transcended those savours, could not, indeed, be of the same nature. Where did it come from? What did it mean? How could I seize and apprehend it?

I drink a second mouthful, in which I find nothing more than in the first, then a third, which gives me rather less. It is time to stop; the potion is losing its virtue. The truth I am seeking lies not in the cup but in myself. The drink has called it into being, but does not know it. I put down the cup and examine my own mind. It alone can discover the truth. But how? What an abyss of uncertainty, when the mind feels overtaken by itself; when it, the seeker, is at the same time the dark region through which it must seek. Seek? More than that: create. It is face to face with something which does not yet exist, which it alone can bring into the light of day.

And I begin again to ask myself what it could have been, this unremembered state which brought with it no proof, in whose presence other states of consciousness melted and vanished. I want to try to make it reappear. I retrace my thoughts to the moment at which I drank the first spoonful of tea. I rediscover the same state, illuminated by no fresh light. I ask my mind to make one further effort, to bring back once more the fleeting sensation. And so that nothing may interrupt it in its course I shut out every obstacle, I stop my ears and screen my attention from the sounds from the next room. And then, feeling that my mind is tiring itself without having any success to report, I compel it for a change to enjoy the distraction which I have just denied it, to think of other things, to rest and refresh itself before making a final effort. And then for the second time I clear an empty space in front of it - I place in position before my mind's eye the still recent taste of that first mouthful, and I feel something start within me, something that leaves its resting place and attempts to rise, something that has been anchored at a great depth; I do not know yet what it is, but I can feel it mounting slowly; I can measure the resistance, I can hear the echo of great spaces traversed.

And suddenly the memory revealed itself. The taste was that of the little piece of madeleine which on Sunday mornings at Combray my aunt Leonie used to give me, dipping it first in her own cup of tea. The sight of the little madeleine had recalled nothing to my mind before I tasted it; perhaps because I had so often seen such things in the meantime, without tasting them, on the trays in pastry-cooks windows, that their image had dissociated itself from those Combray days to take its place among others more recent; perhaps because, of those memories so long abandoned and put out of mind, nothing now survived, everything was scattered; the shapes of things, including that of the little scallop-shell of pastry, so richly sensual under its severe, religious folds, were either obliterated or had been so long dormant as to have lost the power of expansion which would have allowed them to resume their place in my consciousness. But when from a long-distant past nothing subsists, after the people are dead, after the things are broken and scattered, taste and smell alone, more fragile but more enduring, more persistent, more faithful, remain poised a long time, like souls, remembering, waiting, amid the ruins of all the rest; and bear unflinchingly, in the tiny drop of their essence, the vast structure of recollection.

And as soon as I had recognised the taste of the piece of madeleine soaked in her decoction of lime-blossom which my aunt used to give me, immediately the old grey house upon the street, where her room was, rose up like a stage set to attach itself to the little pavilion opening on to the garden; and with the house the town, from morning to night and in all weathers, the Square where I used to be sent before lunch, the streets along which I used to run errands, the country roads we took when it was fine. And as in the game wherein the Japanese amuse themselves by filling a porcelain bowl with water and steeping in it little pieces of paper which until then are without character or form, but, the moment they become wet, stretch and twist and take on colour and distinctive shape, become flowers or houses or people - solid and recognizable - so in that moment all the flowers in our garden and in M Swann's park, and the waterlillies on the Vivonne and the good folk of the village and their little dwellings and the parish church and the whole of Combray and its surroundings sprang into being from my cup of tea.

4

Combray at a distance, from a twenty mile radius, as we used to see it from the railway when we arrived there in the week before Easter, was no more than a church epitomising the town, representing it, speaking for it to the horizon, and as one drew near, gathering close about its long, dark cloak, sheltering from the wind, on the open plain, as a shepherdess gathers her sheep, the wooly grey backs of its huddled houses. Francoise, who had been for many years in my aunt's service and did not at that time suspect that she would one day be transferred entirely to ours, was a little inclined to neglect my aunt during the months we spent there. There had been in my early childhood a time when I knew Francoise so little that on New Year's Day, before going into my great-aunt's dark house, my mother would put a five-franc piece into my hand and say: "Now, be careful. Don't make any mistake. Wait until you hear me say 'Good morning Francoise' and tap you on the arm before you give it to her" No sooner had we arrived in my aunt's dark hall than we saw in the gloom the concentric ripples of a smile of anticipatory gratitude. When we had grown more accustomed to this religious darkness we could discern in her features the disinterested love of humanity, the tender respect for the gentry, which the hope of receiving New Year bounty intensified in the nobler regions of her heart. Since we had begun to go to Combray there was no one I knew better than Francoise. We were her favourites, and in the first years at least she showed for us not only the same consideration as for my aunt, but a keener relish, because we had, in addition to the prestige of belonging to 'the family' the charm of not being her customary employers. And so with what joy she would welcome us, while Mamma inquired after her daughter and her nephews, and if her grandson was a nice boy, and what they were going to do with him, and whether he took after his granny.

And later, when no one else was in the room, Mamma, who knew that Francoise was still mourning for her parents, who had been dead for years, would speak to her kindly about them, asking her endless little questions concerning their lives while the kitchen maid – who made the superior qualities of Francoise shine with added lustre as Error enhances the triumph of Truth- served coffee which was nothing more than hot water, and then carried up to our rooms hot water which was barely luke-warm, I would be lying stretched out on my bed with a book in my hand. My room quivered with the effort to defend its frail, transparent coolness against the afternoon sun behind its almost closed shutters through which, however, a gleam of daylight had contrived to insinuate its golden wings, remaining motionless in a corner between glass and woodwork, like a butterfly poised upon a flower. It was hardly light enough for me to read, and my sense of the day's brightness and splendour was derived solely from the blows struck down below, in the Rue de la Cure, by Camus upon some dusty packing cases.

This dim coolness of my room was to the broad daylight of the street what shadow is to the sunbeam, and presented to my imagination the entire panorama of summer, which my senses, if I had been out walking, could have tasted and enjoyed only piecemeal; and so it was quite in harmony with my state of repose which (thanks to the enlivening adventures related in my books) sustained, like a hand in a stream of running water, the shock and animation of a torrent of activity.

But my grandmother, even if the weather, after growing too hot, had broken, and a storm, or just a shower, had burst over us, would come up and beg me to go outside. And as I did not wish to interrupt my reading, I would go on with it in the garden, under the chestnut tree, in a hooded chair of wicker and canvas in the depths of which I used to sit and feel that I was hidden from the eyes of anyone who might be coming to call upon the family. And then my thoughts, too, formed a similar sort of recess, in the depths of which I felt that I could bury myself and remain invisible even while I looked at what went on outside.

These afternoons were crammed with more dramatic events than occur often in a whole lifetime. These were the events taking place in the book I was reading. It is true that the people concerned in them were not what Francoise would have called 'real people'. But none of the feelings which the joys or misfortunes of a real person arouse in us can be awakened except through a mental picture of those joys or misfortunes; and the ingenuity of the first novelist lay in his understanding that, as the image was the essential element, the suppression, pure and simple, of real people would be a decided improvement. The novelist's happy discovery was substituting for those their equivalent in immaterial sections, that is, which one's soul can assimilate. After which we have made them our own, since it is in ourselves they are happening, as we feverishly turn over the pages of the book. Once the novelist has brought us to this state, in which as in all purely mental states every emotion is multiplied, into which his book comes to disturb us as might a dream, for the space of an hour he sets free within us all the joys and sorrows in the world, a few of which we should have to spend years of life in getting to know, and the most intense of which would never be revealed to us. Next to this would come the landscape, projected before my eyes, in which the story was taking place, which made a far stronger impression than the actual landscape which met my eyes when I raised them. Thus for two summers I sat in the heat of our Combray garden, sick with a longing inspired by the book I was reading. And since there was always lurking in my mind the dream of a woman who would enrich me with her love, that dream in those two summers was quickened with whoever she might be.

Sweet Sunday afternoons beneath the chestnut-tree in the garden at Combray, purged of every commonplace incident of my existence, replaced with a life of adventures and aspirations, you still recall that life to me when I think of - slowly changing and dappled with foliage - your silent, sonorous, fragrant limpid hours.

I would as a rule be left to read in peace. But the interruption and the commentary which a visit from Swann once occasioned in the course of my reading, which had brought me to the work of an author quite new to me – Bergotte – resulted in the consequence that for a long time afterwards it was not against a wall gay with spikes of purple blossom, but against the porch of a Gothic cathedral that I saw the figure of one of the women of whom I dreamed.

For the first few days, like a tune with which one will soon be infatuated but which one has not yet 'got hold of', the things I was to love so passionately in Bergotte's style did not immediately strike me. I could not, it is true, lay down the novel of his which I was reading, but I fancied that I was interested in the subject, as in the dawn of love when we go every day to meet a woman at some party which we think is itself the attraction. Whenever he spoke of something whose beauty had until then remained hidden from me, pine forests or hail storms, Notre Dame Cathedral or *Phedre,* he would make their beauty explode. Realizing the universe contained elements my senses would be powerless to discern did he not bring them within my reach, I longed to have some opinion, some metaphor of his, especially upon such things as I might some day have an opportunity of seeing for myself; and among these particularly some of the historic buildings of France upon certain seascapes, because the emphasis in his books showed that he regarded them as rich in significance and beauty.

When one day I came across in a book by Bergotte some joke about an old family servant which the writer made even more comical, but which was in principle the same joke I had made to my grandmother about Francoise, it was suddenly revealed to me that my own humble existence and the realms of the true were less widely separated than I had supposed, that at certain points they coincided, and I wept upon his printed page as in the arms of a long lost father.

5

One Sunday, while I was reading in the garden, I was interrupted by Swann, who had come to call upon my parents. "What are you reading? May I look?" and seeing how much I seemed to admire Bergotte, Swann, who never spoke at all about the people he knew, said "I know him well. If you would like him to write a few words on the title page of your book I could ask him for you." I dared not accept, but bombarded him with questions about his friend. "Can you tell me, please, who is his favourite actor?"

"Actor? No, I can't say. But I do know this: there's not a man on the stage whom he thinks equal to Berma- he puts her above everyone. Have you seen her?"
"No, Sir, my parents don't allow me to go to the theatre."

"That's a pity. You should insist. Berma in *Phedre*, in the *Cid*; she's only an actress, if you like, but you know I don't believe very much in the 'hierarchy' of the arts." As he spoke I noticed what had often struck me before in his conversations; that whenever he spoke of serious matters, whenever he used an expression which seemed to imply a definite opinion upon some important subject, he would take care to isolate it by using a special intonation, mechanical and ironic, as though he had put the phrase between commas and was anxious to disclaim personal responsibility; "the 'hierarchy', don't you know, as silly people call it." A moment later he went on: "Her acting will give you as noble an inspiration as any masterpiece of art, as – oh, I don't know –" and he laughed, "shall we say the Queens of Chartres?" Until then I supposed this horror of having to give a serious opinion was something Parisian and refined, in contrast to the provincial dogmatism of my grandmother's sister; and I imagined also that it was characteristic of the mental attitude of the circle in which Swann moved. But now I found myself slightly shocked. I thought again of the dinner that night when I had been so unhappy because Mamma would not be coming up to my room, and when he had dismissed the balls given by the Princesse de Leon as being of no importance. And yet it was to just that sort of amusement that he devoted his life. What other life did he set apart for saying what he thought about things?

"Are there any books in which Bergotte has written about Berma?" I asked.

"I think he has, in that little essay on Racine, but it must be out of print. In fact I can ask Bergotte himself next time he comes to dine. He never misses a week, he's my daughter's greatest friend. They go and look at old towns and cathedrals and castles together."

When, that day, I learned that Mlle Swann was a creature living in such rare and fortunate circumstances, bathed in such a sea of privilege that if she should ask her parents whether anyone were coming to dinner she would be answered by those two syllables, radiant with light, by the name of that golden guest who was to her no more than an old friend of the family, Bergotte, that for her the intimate conversation at table, corresponding to what my great aunt's conversation was for me, would be the words of Bergotte on all those subjects which he had not been able to take up in his writings, and on which I should have liked to hear him pronounce his oracles, and that , above all, when she went to visit other towns, he would be walking by her side, unrecognized and glorious, like the gods who came down of old to dwell among mortals – then I realized both the rare worth of a creature such as Mlle Swann and, at the same time, how coarse and ignorant I should appear to her; and I felt so keenly how sweet and how impossible it would be for me to become her friend that I was filled at once with longing and despair.

6

During May we used to go out after dinner to the "Month of Mary" devotions. It was in the Month of Mary that I remember having first fallen in love with hawthorns. Not only were they in the church where, holy ground as it was, we had all of us a right of entry, but arranged upon the altar itself, inseparable from the mysteries in whose celebration they participated, thrusting in among the tapers and the sacred vessels their serried branches, tied to one another horizontally in a stiff, festal scheme of decoration still further embellished by the festoons of leaves, over which were scattered in profusion, as over a bridal train, little clusters of buds of a dazzling whiteness. Thought I dared not look at it except through my fingers, I could sense that this formal scheme was composed of living things, and that it was Nature herself who, by trimming the shape of the foliage, and by adding the crowning ornament of those snowy buds, had made the decorations worthy of what was at once a public rejoicing and a solemn mystery. Higher up on the altar, a flower had opened here and there with a careless grace, holding so unconcernedly, like a final, almost vaporous adornment, its bunch of stamens, slender as gossamer and entirely veiling each corolla, that in following, in trying to mimic to myself the action of their efflorescence, I imagined it as a swift and thoughtless movement of the head, with a provocative glance from her contracted pupils, by a young girl in white, insouciant and vivacious.

M Vinteuil had come in with his daughter and sat down beside us. He belonged to a good family, and had once been piano teacher to my grandmother's sisters, so that when, after losing his wife and inheriting some property, he had retired to the neighborhood of Combray, we used often to invite him to our house. But with his intense prudishness he had given up coming so as not to be obliged to meet Swann, who had made what he called "a most unsuitable marriage."

My mother, on hearing that he composed, told him out of kindness that, when she came to see him, he must play her something of his own. M Vinteuil would have liked nothing better, but he carried politeness and consideration for others to such lengths that he was afraid of boring them, or of appearing egotistical. And every time my mother, in the course of her visit, had returned to the subject he had hurriedly protested and turned the conversation to other topics. His one and only passion was for his daughter and she, with her somewhat boyish appearance, looked so robust that it was hard to restrain a smile when one saw the precautions her father used to take for her health, with spare shawls always in readiness to wrap round her shoulders. My grandmother had drawn our attention to the gentle, delicate, almost timid expression which might often be caught flitting across the freckled face of this otherwise stolid child.

When, before turning to leave the church, I genuflected before the altar, I was suddenly aware of a bittersweet scent of almonds emanating from the hawthorn-blossom, and I then noticed on the flowers themselves little patches of a creamier colour, beneath which I imagined this scent must lie concealed, as the taste of an almond cake lay beneath the burned parts, or that of Mlle Vinteuil's cheeks beneath their freckles. Despite the motionless silence of the hawthorns, this intermittent odor came to me like the murmuring of an intense organic life with which the whole altar was quivering like a hedgerow explored by living antennae, of which I was reminded by some stamens, almost red in color, which seemed to have kept the springtime virulence, the power of stinging insects now flowers.

If it was a moonlit night and warm my father, in his thirst for glory, instead of taking us home at once would lead us on a long walk round by the Calvary, which my mother's incapacity for taking her bearings made her regard as a triumph of his genius. Sometimes we would go as far as the viaduct, whose long stone strides began at the railway station and to me typified all the wretchedness of exile beyond the last outposts of civilization, because every year as we came down from Paris we were warned to take special care not to miss the station, to be ready before the train stopped, since it would start again in two minutes and proceed across the viaduct out of the lands of Christendom, of which Combray, to me, represented the furthest limit. We would return by the Boulevard de la Gare, which contained the most attractive villas in the town. In each of their gardens the moonlight, copying the art of Hubert Robert, scattered its broken staircases of white marble, its fountains, its iron gates temptingly ajar. Its beams had swept away the telegraph office. All that was left of it was a column, half shattered but preserving the beauty of a ruin which endures for all time. I would by now be dragging my weary limbs and ready to drop with sleep; the balmy scent of the lime-trees seemed a reward that could be won only at the price of fatigue and not worth the effort. From gates far apart the watchdogs, awakened by our steps in the silence, would set up an antiphonal barking such as I still hear at times of an evening, and among which the Boulevard de la Gare (when the public gardens of Combray were constructed on its site) must have taken refuge. For wherever I may be, as soon as they begin their alternate challenge and response, I can see it again with its lime-trees, it's pavement glistening beneath the moon.

Suddenly my father would bring us to a standstill and ask my mother – Where are we? Exhausted by the walk but still proud of her husband, she would lovingly confess she had not the least idea. He would shrug his shoulders. And then, as though he had produced it with his latchkey from his waistcoat pocket, he would point out to us the back gate of our own garden. My mother would murmur admiringly "You really are wonderful!" And from that instant I did not have to take another step; the ground moved forward under my feet in that garden where for so long my actions had ceased to require control from my will. Habit had come to take me in her arms and carry me all the way to my bed like a child.

At the beginning of the season, when the days ended early, we would still be able to see, as we turned into the Rue du Saint-Esprit, a reflection of the setting sun in the windows of the house and a band of crimson beyond the timbers of the Calvary, which was mirrored further on in the pond; a fiery glow that, accompanied often by a sharp tang in the air, would associate itself in my mind with the glow of the fire over which, at that very moment, was roasting the chicken that was to furnish me, in the place of the poetic pleasure of the walk, with the sensual pleasures of good feeding, warmth and rest. But in summer, when we came back to the house, the sun would not have set; and while we were upstairs paying our visit to aunt Leonie its rays, sinking until they lay along her window-sill, would be caught and held by the large inner curtains and the loops which tied them back to the wall, and then would illuminate the room with a delicate, slanting, woodland glow. But on some days, though very rarely, the pond beneath the Calvary would have lost its fiery glow, while a long ribbon of moonlight, gradually broadening and splintered by every ripple upon the water's surface, would stretch across it from end to end. Then, as we drew near the house, we would see a figure standing upon the doorstep, and Mamma would say to me: "Good heavens! There's Francoise looking out for us; your aunt must be anxious; that means we're late."

And without wasting time by stopping to take off our things we would dash upstairs to my aunt Leonie's room to reassure her, to prove to her by our bodily presence that all her gloomy imaginings were false, that nothing had happened to us, but that we had gone the Guermantes way and when one took that walk, why, my aunt knew well enough that one could never be sure what time one would be home.

For there were, in the environs of Combray, two "ways" which we used to take for our walks, and they were so diametrically opposed that we would actually leave the house by a different door according to the way we had chosen: the way towards Meseglise-la-Vineuse, which we also called Swann's way because to get there one had to pass along the boundary of M Swann's estate, and the Guermantes way. When we had decided to go the Meseglise way we would start from the front door of my aunt's house, which opened on to the Rue du Saint-Esprit. We would be greeted by the gunsmith, drop our letters into the box, tell Theodore, from Francoise, as we passed that she had run out of oil or coffee, and we would leave the town by the road which ran along the white fence of M. Swann's park. Before reaching it we would be met on our way by the scent of his lilac trees, come out to welcome strangers. From amid the fresh little green hearts of their foliage they raised inquisitively over the fence of the park their plumes of white or mauve blossom which glowed, even in the shade, with the sunlight in which they bathed. Some of them, half concealed by the little tiled house known as the Archers' Lodge in which Swann's keeper lived, overtopped its Gothic gable with their pink minaret. Despite my desire to throw my arms about their pliant forms and to draw down towards me the starry locks that crowned their fragrant heads, we would pass them by without stopping, for my parents had ceased to visit Tansonville since Swann's marriage and, so as not to appear to be looking into his park, instead of taking the path which skirted his property and then climbed straight up to the open fields, we took another path which led in the same direction, but circuitously, and brought us out beyond it.

One day my grandfather said to my father "Don't you remember Swann telling us yesterday that his wife and daughter had gone off to Rheims and that he was spending a day or two in Paris? We might go along by the park, since the ladies are not at home; that will make it a little shorter".

We stopped for a moment by the fence. The absence of Mlle Swann which – since it preserved me from the terrible risk of seeing her appear on one of the paths, and of being identified and scorned by this privileged little girl who had Bergotte for a friend and used to go with him to visit cathedrals - made the exploration of Tansonville, now for the first time permissible, a matter of indifference to myself, seemed on the contrary to invest the property, in my grandfather's and my father's eyes, with an added attraction. I should have liked to see, by a miracle, Mlle Swann appear with her father, so close to us that we should not have time to avoid her, and to make her acquaintance. And so, when I suddenly noticed a straw basket lying forgotten on the grass by the side of a fishing line whose float was bobbing in the water, I made every effort to keep my father and grandfather looking in another direction, away from this sign that she might, after all, be in residence. The sunlight fell from a motionless sky and even the water, dreaming no doubt of some imaginary maelstrom, intensified the sight of that floating cork; now almost vertical, it seemed on the point of plunging down out of sight, and I had begun to wonder whether, setting aside the longing and the terror that I had of making her acquaintance, it was not actually my duty to warn Mlle Swann that the fish was biting – when I was obliged to run after my father and grandfather who were calling me, surprised I had not followed them along the little path leading up to the open fields. I found the whole path throbbing with the fragrance of hawthorn-blossom. The hedge resembled a series of chapels, whose walls were no longer visible under mountains of flowers heaped upon their altars; while beneath them the sun cast a checquered light upon the ground, as though it had just passed through a stained glass window; and the flowers, themselves adorned also, held out each its little bunch of glittering stamens with an absent minded air, like those which, in the church, framed the stairway or the mullions of the windows.

But it was in vain that I lingered beside the hawthorns - breathing in their odor, trying to fix it in my mind, losing it, recapturing it, absorbing myself in the rhythm which disposed the flowers - they went on offering me the same charm without letting me delve any more deeply. I turned away from them for a moment to return to them afresh. My eyes traveled up the bank which rose steeply to the fields beyond the hedge, alighting on a stray poppy or a few laggard cornflowers which decorated the slope here and there like the border of a tapestry whereon may be glimpsed sporadically the theme which will emerge in the panel itself; infrequent still, spaced out like the scattered houses which herald the approach of a village, they betokened to me the vast expanse of waving corn beneath the fleecy clouds, and the sight of a single poppy hoisting upon its slender rigging and holding against the breeze its scarlet ensign made my heart beat like that of a traveler who glimpses on some low lying ground a stranded boat which is being caulked and cries out, although he has not yet caught sight of it, "The Sea!"

And then I returned to the hawthorns but in vain did I concentrate upon the flowers, the feeling they aroused remained obscure and vague, struggling and failing to free itself, to float across and become one with them. And then, inspiring me with that rapture which we feel on seeing a work by our favourite painter quite different from those we already know or, better still, when a piece of music we have heard on the piano appears to us clothed in all the colours of the orchestra, my grandfather called, pointing to the Tansonville hedge, "You're fond of hawthorns; just look at this pink one – isn't it lovely?" And it was indeed a hawthorn, but one whose blossom was pink and lovelier even than the white. Embedded in the hedge, but as different from it as a young girl in festal attire among a crowd of dowdy women in everyday clothes, it glowed there, smiling in its fresh pink garments.

The hedge afforded a glimpse, inside the park, of an alley bordered with jasmine, pansies, and verbenas while a long green hose, coiling across the gravel, sent up from its sprinkler a prismatic fan. Suddenly I stood still, unable to move. A little girl with fair, reddish hair, who appeared to be returning from a walk, and held a spade in her hand, was looking at us, raising a face powdered with pinkish freckles. Her black eyes gleamed, and since I did not at that time know, and indeed have never learned, how to reduce a strong impression to its elements, for a long time afterwards the memory of those bright eyes would present itself to me as azure since her complexion was fair; so much so that, if her eyes had not been so black – which was what struck one most on first seeing her – I should not have been so especially enamoured of their imagined blue. I gazed at her, first with that gaze at whose window all the senses lean out, a gaze eager to reach the body at which it is aimed, and the soul with the body; then with another unconsciously imploring look, to force her to pay attention to me. She cast a glance forwards and sideways, to take stock of my grandfather and my father, and turned away with an indifferent air; and while they, continuing to walk on without noticing her, overtook me, she went on staring out of the corner of her eye in my direction without appearing to see me, but with a half hidden smile which I could only interpret as a mark of contempt.

"Gilberte, come along; what are you doing?" called out a lady in white whom I had not seen until that moment while, a little way beyond her, a gentleman in a suit of linen stared at me. The little girl's smile faded and, seizing her spade, she made off without turning to look again in my direction. Thus was wafted to my ears the name of Gilberte, whereas the moment before she had been merely an uncertain image. So it came to me with the mystery of the happy beings who lived and walked and travelled in her company; unfolding beneath the arch of the pink hawthorn, and with the unknown world of her existence into which I should never penetrate.

For a moment (as we moved away and my

grandfather murmured: "Poor Swann, what a life they are leading him-sending him away so she can be alone with Charlus-I recognized him at once! And the child, too; at her age, to be mixed up in all that!") the impression left on me by the tone in which Gilberte's mother had spoken to her without her answering back, her being obliged to obey someone else, as not being superior to the whole world, calmed my anguish somewhat, revived some hope in me, and cooled the ardour of my love. I loved her; I was sorry not to have had the time and the inspiration to insult her, to hurt her, to force her to keep some memory of me. I thought her so beautiful that I should have liked to shake my fist at her and shout "I think you're hideous, grotesque; how I loathe you!" But I walked away, carrying with me, then and forever, as the first illustration of a type of happiness inaccessible to a little boy of my kind, the picture of a little girl with reddish hair and freckled skin, who held a spade in her hand and smiled as she directed a long, sly stare. Already her name was beginning to perfume everything with which it had any association; her grandparents, whom mine had the good fortune to know, the profession of stockbroker, the melancholy neighborhood of the Champs-Elysees, where she lived in Paris.

Once in the fields we never left them again during our Meseglise walk. They were perpetually traversed by the wind, as though by an invisible wanderer. Every year, on the day of our arrival, in order to feel that I really was at Combray, I would climb the hill to greet it as it swept me along in its wake. One always had the wind for companion when one went the Meseglise way, on that gently undulating plain where for mile after mile it met no rising ground. I knew that Mlle Swann used often to go and spend a few days at Laon and when, on hot afternoons, I saw a breath of wind emerge from the furthest horizon, bowing the heads of the corn in distant fields, pouring like a flood over that vast expanse and finally come to rest, warm and rustling, among the clover at my feet, that plain which was common to us both seemed to unite us. I would imagine the same breath of wind had passed close to her and I would kiss it.

On my left was a village called Champieu. On my right I could see across the cornfields the two chiseled rustic spires of Saint Andre des Champs, themselves as tapering as two ears of wheat. At regular intervals the apple trees opened their broad petals of white satin, or dangled the shy bunches of their blushing buds. It was on the Meseglise way that I first noticed the circular shadow which apple trees cast upon the sunlit ground, and also those threads of golden silk which the setting sun weaves slantingly downwards from their leaves, and which I used to see my father slash through with his stick. Sometimes in the afternoon sky the moon would creep up, white as a cloud, furtive, lustreless, suggesting an actress who does not have to come on for a while, and watches the rest of the company for a moment from the auditorium, not wishing to attract attention to herself.

It was along the Meseglise way, at Montjouvain, a house built on the edge of a large pond against the side of a steep, bushy hill, that M Vinteuil lived, and so we used often to meet his daughter driving at full speed along the road. After a certain year we never saw her alone, but always accompanied by a friend, a girl older than herself with a bad reputation in the neighborhood, who one day installed herself permanently at

Montjouvain. People said: "That poor M Vinteuil must be blinded by fatherly love not to see what everyone is talking about-a man who is shocked by the slightest loose word letting his daughter bring a woman like that to live under his roof! He says that she is a most superior woman with a heart of gold, and that she would have shown extraordinary musical talent if she had only been trained. He may be sure it isn't music that she's teaching his daughter."

One day, when we were walking with Swann, M Vinteuil, turning out of another street, found himself so suddenly face to face with us all that he had no time to escape and Swann conversed at great length with M Vinteuil, with whom for a long time he had been barely on speaking terms, and invited him, before leaving us, to send his daughter over one day to play at Tansonville. It was an invitation which, two years earlier, would have incensed M Vinteuil, but which now filled him with so much gratitude that he felt obliged to refrain from accepting. Swann's friendly regard for his daughter seemed to him to be so honorable that he felt it would perhaps be advisable not to make use of it, so as to have the wholly Platonic satisfaction of preserving it.

"What a charming man!" he said to us, after Swann had gone, "What a pity that he should have made such a deplorable marriage!" And then, so strong an element of hypocrisy is there in even the most sincere people, who lay aside the opinion they actually hold of a person while they are talking to him and express it as soon as he is no longer there, my family joined with M Vinteuil in deploring Swann's marriage, invoking principles and convention which they appeared to suggest were in no way infringed at Montjouvain.

If the weather was bad all morning, my parents would abandon the idea of a walk, and I would remain at home. But later on I formed the habit of going out by myself on such days, and walking towards Meseglise la Combray to settle my aunt Leonie's estate; for she had died at last. That autumn my parents, so preoccupied with all the legal formalities, the discussions with solicitors, and tenants that they had little time to make excursions, began to let me go for walks without them along the Meseglise way, wrapped up in a huge plaid which protected me from the rain and which I was all the more ready to throw over my shoulders because i felt that its tartan stripes scandalised Francoise, whom it was impossible to convince that the color of one's clothes had nothing to do with one's mourning, and to whom the grief which we had shown on my aunt's death was wholly inadequate.

My walks were all the more delightful because I used to take them after long hours spent over a book. When I was tired of reading I would throw my plaid across my shoulders and set out; my body, which in a long spell of enforced immobility had stored up vital energy, now felt the need, like a spinning top wound up and let go, to expend it in every direction. The walls of houses, the Tansonville hedge, the bushes adjoining Montjouvain all must bear the blows of my walking stick or umbrella, must hear my shouts of happiness, these being no more than expressions of the confused ideas which exhilarated me. Thus it is most of our attempts to translate our innermost feelings do no more than relieve us of them by drawing them out in a form which does not help us to identify them. When I try to reckon all that I owe to the Meseglise way, all the discoveries of which it was either the setting or cause, I am reminded it was in that same autumn, near the slope which overlooks Montjouvain, that I was struck for the first time by this discordance between our impressions and their expression. After an hour of rain and wind, against which I had struggled cheerfully, as I came to the edge of the Montjouvain pond, beside a little hut with a tiled roof in which M Vinteuil's gardener kept his tools, the sun had just reappeared and its golden rays, washed clean by the shower, glittered anew in the sky, on the trees, on the wall of the hut and the wet tiles of the roof – on the ridge of which a hen was strutting. The wind tugged at the wild grass growing from cracks in the wall and at the hen's downy feathers, which floated out to their full extent. The tiled roof cast upon the pond, translucent again in the sunlight, a dappled pink reflection which I had never observed before. Seeing upon the water and the surface of the wall a pallid smile responding to the smiling sky, I cried aloud, brandishing my furled umbrella: "Gosh gosh gosh!" But at the same time I felt I was duty bound not to content myself with these words but to see more clearly into my rapture.

And it was at that moment too – thanks to a peasant who went past, apparently in a bad humour already but more so when he nearly got a poke in the face from my umbrella, and who replied somewhat coolly to my "Fine day!" that I learned identical emotions do not spring up simultaneously in the hearts of all men. Later on, when a long spell of reading had put me in a mood for conversation, the friend to whom I was longing to talk would have wanted to be left undisturbed, and if I had been thinking of my parents with affection they would discover some misdeed and scold me severely as I was about to fling myself into their arms.

If the Meseglise way was fairly easy, it was a different matter when we took the Guermantes way for that meant a long walk and we must first make sure of the weather. When my father had received the same favourable reply from the gardener and the barometer in succession, then someone would say at dinner: Tomorrow, if the weather holds, we might go the Guermantes way. And off we would set, immediately after lunch, through the little garden gate into the Rue des Perchamps, narrow and bent at a sharp angle, dotted with clumps of grass among which two or three wasps would spend the day botanising, a street as quaint as its name, a street for which one might search in vain today, for the village school now occupies its site.

The great charm of the Guermantes way was that we had beside us, almost all the time, the Vivonne. We crossed it first, ten minutes after leaving the house, by a footbridge called the pont-Vieux. Every year when we arrived, on Easter Sunday I would run there to see the river flowing past, its only companions a clump of premature daffodils and early primroses, while here and there burned the blue flame of a violet, its stem drooping beneath the weight of the drop of perfume stored in its tiny horn. The pont-Vieux led to a tow path, beneath which a fisherman in a straw hat seemed to have taken root. He must have known my family for he used to raise his hat when we passed; and then I would be just on the point of asking his name when someone would signal me to keep quiet or I would frighten the fish. We would follow the tow path, which ran along a steep bank above the stream. The bank on the other side was lower, stretching in a series of meadows as far as the village and the distant railway station. Over these were strewn the remains, half buried in the long grass, of the castle of the old Counts of Combray who, during the Middle Ages, had the Vivonne as a barrier against attack from the Lords of Guermantes and Abbots of Martinville. Nothing was left now but a few barely visible stumps of towers, hummocks upon the broad surface of the fields, and a few broken battlements from which, in their day, the crossbowmen had hurled their missiles and the watchmen had gazed out over Novepont, Clairefontaine, Martinville-le-sec, Bailleau-l'Exempt; fiefs all of them of Guermantes by which Combray was hemmed in, but now razed to the level of the grass and overrun by the boys from the lay brothers' school who came there for study or recreation. A past that had almost sunk into the ground, lying by the water's edge like an idler taking the air, yet giving me much food for thought, making the name of Combray connote to me an historic city vastly different, gripping my imagination by the remote features which it half concealed beneath a spangled veil of buttercups. For the buttercups grew past numbering in this spot which they had chosen for their games among the grass, standing singly, in couples, in whole companies, yellow as the yolk of eggs, and glowing with added lustre, potent enough to produce an effect of absolute, purposeless beauty; and so it had been from my earliest childhood, when from the towpath I had stretched out my arms towards them before I could even properly spell their charming name – a name fit for the Prince in some fairy tale – immigrants, perhaps, from Asia centuries ago but naturalised now for ever in the village, rejoicing in the sunshine and the water's edge, faithful to their little glimpse of the railway station.

Presently the course of the Vivonne became choked with water plants. At first they appeared singly – a lily for instance, which the current would never leave at rest. But further on the current slackened so that the little ponds into which the Vivonne was diverted were aflower with water-lilies. After leaving this the Vivonne began to flow again more swiftly. How often have I watched, and longed to imitate when I should be free to lie as I chose, a rower who had shipped his oars and lay flat in the bottom of his boat, letting it drift with the current, seeing nothing but the sky gliding slowly by above him, his face aglow with happiness and peace.

We would sit down among the irises at the water's edge. In the holiday sky an idle cloud dawdled. From time to time, oppressed by boredom, a carp would heave itself out of the water with an anxious gasp. Before starting home we would sit there for a long time, eating fruit and bread and chocolate, on the grass over which came to us, faint, horizontal, but dense and metallic still, echoes of the bells of Saint-Hilaire, which had not melted into the air they had traversed for so long and, ribbed by their sound waves, throbbed as they grazed the flowers at our feet.

Never in the course of our walks along the Guermantes way were we able to penetrate as far as the source of the Vivonne, which had in my mind so abstract, so ideal an existence that I had been as surprised when someone told me it was actually in the same department, a number of miles from Combray, as I had been when I learned there was another point somewhere on earth where, according to the ancients, opened the jaws of Hell. Nor could we ever get as far as that other goal which I so longed to reach, Guermantes itself. I knew it was the residence of the Duc and Duchesse de Guermantes, I knew they were personages who did actually exist, but whenever I thought about them I pictured them in tapestry, like the Comtesse de Guermantes which hung in our church. I used to dream that Mme de Guermantes, taking a sudden fancy to me, invited me there. And when evening came, holding my hand in hers, as we passed by the little gardens of her vassals she would point out to me the flowers that leaned their red and purple spikes along the tops of the low walls and would teach me all their names. She would make me tell her, too all about the poems I intended to compose. And these dreams reminded me that, since I wished to become a writer, it was high time to decide what sort of books I was going to write. But as soon as I asked myself the question, and tried to discover some subject to which I could impart significance, my mind would stop like a clock, I would feel either that I was wholly devoid of talent or that perhaps some malady of the brain was hindering its development. And so, utterly despondent, I renounced literature for ever.

7

One day my mother said to me: "You're always talking about Mme de Guermantes. Well Dr Percepied took great care of her when she was ill and so she's coming to Combray for his daughter's wedding. You'll be able to see her in church." It was from Dr Percepied, as it happened, that I had heard about Mme de Guermantes, and he had even shown us an illustrated paper in which she was depicted in the costume she had worn at a fancy dress ball.

During the nuptial mass the verger, by moving to one side, enabled me to see in one of the chapels a fair-haired lady with a large nose, piercing blue eyes, a billowy scarf of mauve silk, and a little pimple at the corner of her nose. I remembered having heard it said that this chapel was reserved for the Guermantes family, whenever any of its members came to attend a ceremony at Combray; hence there only one woman resembling the portrait of Mme de Guermantes who on that day could conceivably be sitting in that chapel. And then – oh marvelous independence of the human gaze, tied to the human face by a cord so loose, so long, so elastic that it can stray alone as far as it may choose-while Mme de Guermantes sat in the chapel above the tombs of her dead ancestors, her gaze wandered here and there, rose to the capitals of the pillars, and even rested momentarily upon myself, like a ray of sunlight straying down the nave, but a ray of sunlight which, at the moment when I received its caress, appeared conscious of where it fell. And my eyes resting upon her fair hair, her blue eyes, the lines of her neck, I cried out within myself as I admired this deliberately unfinished sketch: "How lovely she is! What true nobility! It is indeed a proud Guermantes, the descendant of Genevieve de Brabant, that I have before me!" And the attention which I focused on her face succeeded in isolating it so completely that today, when I call that marriage ceremony to mind, I find it impossible to visualise any single person who was present except her, and at once I fell in love with her, for if it is sometimes enough to make us love a woman that she should look on us with contempt, as I supposed Mlle Swann to have done, and that we should think that she can never be ours, sometimes, too, it is enough that she should look on us kindly, and that we should think of her as almost ours already.

How often, after that day, in the course of my walks along the Guermantes way, did I reflect on my lack of qualification for a literary career, and abandon all hope of ever becoming a famous author. The regrets I felt for this made me suffer so acutely that, in order to banish them, my mind ceased entirely to think of verse-making, fiction, the poetic future my lack of talent precluded me from. Then, quite independently of all these preoccupations and in no way connected with them, suddenly a roof, a gleam of sunlight on a stone, the smell of a path would make me stop still to enjoy the pleasure each of them gave me, and also because they appeared to be concealing something which they invited me to come and take but which I never managed to discover. Once, however, when we had prolonged our walk and so had been glad to be overtaken half-way home, as afternoon darkened into evening, by Dr Percepied who had recognised us and made us jump in, I received an impression of this sort which I did not abandon without getting to the bottom of it to some extent. I had been set on the box beside the coachman and we were going like the wind because the doctor had still to see a patient at whose door we should wait for him. At a bend in the road I experienced pleasure on catching sight of the twin steeples of Martinville, bathed in the setting sun and constantly changing their position with the movement of the carriage and the windings of the road, and then of a third steeple, that of Vieuxvicq which appeared to be standing by their side. In noticing the shape of their spires and their shifting lines I felt something more lay behind, something which they seemed at once to contain and conceal. A few minutes later we drew up outside the Church. I got down from the box to talk to my parents while we waited for the doctor. Then it was time to set off again and I resumed my seat, turning my head to look back once more at the steeples. The coachman having barely acknowledged my remarks I was obliged, in default of other conversation, to fall back on my own and to attempt to recapture the vision of my steeples. And presently their outlines and their sunlit surfaces peeled away; something of what they had concealed from me became apparent; a thought came into my mind, framing itself in words in my head; and I could no longer think of anything else. I borrowed a pencil and some paper from the doctor, and in spite of the jolting of the carriage, composed the following little fragment.

Alone, rising from the level of the plain, and seemingly lost in that expanse of open country, the twin steeples of Martinville rose towards the sky. Presently we saw three: springing into position in front of them with a bold leap a third, dilatory steeple had come to join them. The minutes passed, we were travelling fast, and yet the three steeples were always a long way ahead of us, like three birds perched upon the plain. Then the steeple of Vieuxvicq drew aside, and the steeples of Martinville remained alone, gilded by the light of the setting sun. We had been so long in approaching them that I was thinking of the time that must still elapse before we could reach them when, of a sudden, the carriage turned a corner and set us down at their feet; and they had flung themselves so abruptly in our path we had barely time to stop before being dashed against the porch. We resumed our journey. A little later, when we were already close to Combray, I caught sight of them for the last time, far away, seeming no more than three flowers painted above the low line of the fields and after some awkward, stumbling movements of their noble silhouettes, drawing close to one another, gliding one behind another, forming now against the rosy sky no more than a single dusky shape, charming and resigned, and vanishing in the night.

At the moment when, in the corner of the box seat where the doctor's coachman was in the habit of stowing the poultry he bought, I had finished writing, I was so filled with happiness, I felt it had so entirely relieved my mind of its obsession with the steeples that, as though I myself were a hen and had just laid an egg, I began to sing at the top of my voice.

So the Meseglise way and the Guermantes way remain for me linked with many of the little incidents of the life of the mind. The flowers which played then among the grass, the water which rippled past in the sunshine, the whole landscape still lingers around the memory and the scent of hawthorn which flits along the hedge, a sound of echoless footsteps on a gravel path, a bubble formed against the side of a waterplant by the current of the stream – all these my mind has borne along with it and kept alive through the years, while around them the paths have vanished and those who trod them, and even the memory of those who trod them, are dead. It is as the deepest layer of my mental soil, as the firm ground on which I still stand, that I regard the Meseglise and Guermantes ways. It is because I believed in things and in people while I walked along those paths that the things and the people they made known to me are the only ones that still bring me joy. Whether because the faith which creates has ceased to exist in me, or because reality takes shape in memory alone, the flowers that people show me now never seem to be true flowers. The Meseglise way with its lilacs, its hawthorns, its cornflowers, its poppies, its apple trees, the Guermantes way with its river full of tadpoles, its waterlilies and its buttercups, constituted for me for all time the image of the landscape in which I should like to live. And I would not be satisfied were I led to the banks of a river in which there were water-lilies more beautiful than those in the Vivonne, any more than I should have wished for a mother more beautiful than my own to come and say good night to me. What I want to see again is the Guermantes way as I knew it, with the farm that stood a little apart from the two neighbouring farms at the entrance to the oak avenue; those meadows in which, when they are burnished by the sun to the luminescence of a pond, the leaves of the apple trees are reflected; that whole landscape grips me sometimes at night, in my dreams, with a power of which I can discover no trace when I awake.

No doubt, by virtue of having united so many different impressions in my mind, the Meseglise and Guermantes ways left me exposed, in later life, to disillusionment and mistakes. But by the same token they give a significance which is for me alone. When, on a summer evening, the sky growls like a tawny lion, and everyone is complaining of the storm, it is the memory of the Meseglise way that makes me stand alone in ecstasy, inhaling, through the noise of the falling rain, the lingering scent of invisible lilacs.

Thus I would often lie until morning, dreaming of the old days at Combray, of my melancholy and wakeful evenings there, of other days besides, the memory of which had been more recently restored to me by the taste of a cup of tea and, by an association of memories, of a story which, many years after I had left the little place, had been told me of a love affair in which Swann had been involved before I was born.

8 - SWANN IN LOVE

To admit you to the "little nucleus" the "little group", the "little clan" at the Verdurins', one condition sufficed but that one was indispensable: Each new recruit whom the Verdurins failed to persuade that the evenings spent by other people, in other houses than theirs, were as dull as ditch-water, saw himself banished forthwith. Women being in this respect more rebellious than men, more reluctant to lay aside all curiousity and the desire to find out whether other salons might be entertaining, the Verdurins had been obliged to expel, one after another, all those of the "faithful" who were female. Apart from the doctor's young wife, they were reduced almost exclusively that season to a young woman almost of the demi-monde, a Mme de Crecy, whom Mme Verdurin called by her Christian name, Odette.

Now there was nothing whatsoever in common between the "little nucleus" and the society which Swann frequented, and true socialites would have thought it hardly worth while to occupy so exceptional a position in the fashionable world in order to end up with an introduction to the Verdurins. But Swann was so fond of women that he did not make an effort to find attractive the women with whom he spent his time, but sought to spend his time with women whom he found attractive. And as often as not they were women whose beauty was of a distinctly vulgar type. Depth of character, or a melancholy expression, would freeze his senses, which were however instantly aroused at the sight of healthy, abundant, rosy flesh.

When one evening at the theatre he was introduced to Odette de Crecy by an old friend of his who had spoken of her as a ravishing creature with whom he might come to an understanding, she had struck Swann not, certainly, as being devoid of beauty, but as endowed with a kind of beauty which left him indifferent. Some time after this introduction she had written to ask Swann whether she might see his collections, and when he allowed her to come she had said to him as she left how sorry she was to have stayed so short a time, speaking of him as though he had meant something more to her than the rest of the people she knew, and appearing to establish a kind of bond which had made him smile. At the time of life, tinged with disenchantment, which Swann was approaching, when a man can content himself with being in love for the pleasure of loving without expecting too much in return, this mutual sympathy may well become the cause of love if it manifests itself. In his younger days a man dreams of possessing the heart of the woman whom he loves; later the feeling that he possesses a woman's heart may be enough to make him fall in love.

Odette de Crecy came again to see Swann; her visits grew more frequent, and doubtless each visit revived the sense of disappointment which he felt at the sight of a face whose details he had somewhat forgotten. But after Odette had left him, Swann would think with a smile of her telling how the time would drag until he allowed her to come again; he remembered the anxious, timid way in which she had begged him that it might not be too long, and the way she had gazed at him then. He had pleaded the pressure of work, an essay – which in reality he had abandoned years ago – on Vermeer of Delft. "I know I'm quite useless" she had replied, and yet I should so much like to learn, you'll only laugh at me but this painter who stops you from seeing me, I've never even heard of him; is he alive still? Can I see any of his things in Paris, to have some idea of what's going on behind that great brow, to be able to say 'There, that's what he's thinking about!'"

He had excused himself on the grounds of his fear of forming new friendships, which he gallantly described as his fear of being made unhappy. "You're afraid of affection? How odd, when I go about seeking nothing else, and would give my soul to find it!" she had said, so naturally and with such conviction he had been genuinely touched. "Some woman must have made you suffer. And you think the rest are like her. She can't have understood you're such an exceptional person. That's what I liked about you from the start; you weren't like everybody else. Do you know what would be nice – if I were to introduce you to Mme Verdurin, where I go every evening. Just fancy our meeting there, and my thinking that it was a little for my sake that you had come."

The Verdurins had dining with them, on the day when Swann made his first appearance, Dr and Mme Cottard, the young pianist and his aunt, and the painter then in favour. These were joined, in the course of the evening, by a few more of the "faithful." Odette had gone to sit on a tapestry-covered settee near the piano, saying to Mme Verdurin "I have my own little corner, haven't I?" And Mme Verdurin, seeing Swann by himself on a chair, made him get up: "You're not at all comfortable there. Go along and sit by Odette. You can make room for M Swann there, can't you Odette?"

"What charming Beauvais!" said Swann politely, stopping to admire the settee before he sat down on it. "Ah! I'm glad you appreciate my settee" replied Mme Verdurin, "and I warn you that if you expect ever to see another like it you may as well abandon the idea at once. Some people go to Fontainebleau for cures; I take my own little Beauvais cure here. But, M Swann, you mustn't run away without feeling the little bronze mouldings on the back. Isn't it an exquisite patina? No, no you must feel them properly, with your whole hand!"

"If Mme Verdurin is going to start fingering her bronzes" said the painter "we shan't get any music tonight"

"Be quiet you wretch! And yet we poor women" she went on, turning towards Swann, "are forbidden pleasures far less voluptuous than this. There is no flesh in the world to compare with it. None. When M. Verdurin did me the honor of being madly jealous...come, you might at least be polite – don't say that you've never been jealous!"

"But my dear, I've said absolutely nothing. Look here, Doctor, I call you as a witness. Did I utter a word?"

Swann had begun, out of politeness, to finger the bronzes, and did not like to stop.

"Come along, you can caress them later. Now it's you who are going to be caressed, aurally. You'll like that, I think. Here's the young gentleman who will take charge of that."

After the pianist had played, Swann was even more affable towards him than towards any of the other guests, for the following reason:

The year before, at an evening party, he had heard a piece of music played on the piano and violin. At first he had appreciated only the material quality of the sounds. And it had been a keen pleasure when, below the delicate line of the violin, slender but robust, compact and commanding, he had suddenly become aware of the mass of the piano beginning to emerge in a sort of liquid rippling, smooth yet restless, like the tumult of the sea, silvered and charmed into a minor key by the moonlight. Without being able to give a name to what was pleasing him, suddenly enraptured, he had tried to grasp the phrase or harmony that had just been played and had opened and expanded his soul, as the fragrance of roses has the power of dilating nostrils. Perhaps it was owing to his ignorance of music that he received so confused an impression, one of those none the less purely musical impressions, limited, original and irreducible. Doubtless the notes we hear at such moments tend, according to their pitch and volume, to spread out over surfaces, to trace arabesques, to give us the sensation of breadth or caprice. But the notes themselves have vanished before these sensations have developed sufficiently to escape those which the succeeding or even simultaneous notes have already begun to awaken in us. And this impression would continue in its ceaseless overlapping, the motifs barely discernible, to plunge again and disappear and drown, recognized only by the pleasure they instill, impossible to describe, to recollect, to name – did not our memory enable us to compare them with those that follow. And so, scarcely had the sensation which Swann had experienced died away, before his memory had furnished him with a transcript, sketchy it is true, and provisional, which he had been able to glance at while the piece continued, so that when the same impression returned it was no longer impossible to grasp. He could picture its extent, he had before him something that was no longer pure music, but rather architecture, and which allowed the actual music to be recalled. This time he had distinguished a phrase which emerged for a few moments above the waves of sound. It had suggested to him a world of delights, of whose existence he had never dreamed, and he had been filled with love for it, as with a new and strange desire. When he returned home he felt the need of it: he was like a man into whose life a woman passing by has brought the image of beauty which deepens his own sensibility, although he does not know her name or whether he will see her again.

Indeed this passion for a phrase of music seemed, for a time, to open up before Swann the possibility of a sort of rejuvenation. He had so long ceased to direct his life towards any goal, confining himself to the pursuit of satisfactions, that he had come to believe, without ever admitting it, that he would remain in that condition for the rest of his days. More than this, since his mind no longer entertained ideas, he had ceased to believe in their reality. Thus he had grown into the habit of taking refuge in trivial considerations, which enabled him to disregard matters of fundamental importance. He would be extremely precise about the recipe for a dish, the date of a painter's birth, and titles of his works. Sometimes, in spite of himself, he would go so far as to express an opinion on a work of art, but then he would cloak his words in a tone of irony, as though he did not altogether associate himself with what he was saying. But now Swann found in himself, in the memory of the phrase he had heard, in certain other sonatas which he made people play to see whether he might not perhaps discover his phrase therein, the presence of one of those realities which he had ceased to believe and he was conscious again of the desire and almost the strength to consecrate his life. But, never having managed to find out whose work it was that he had heard that evening, he had been unable to procure a copy and had finally forgotten the quest. He had encountered several people who had been at the party, but most of them had either arrived after or left before the piece was played; some had gone into another room to talk. As for his hosts they knew it was a recent work which the musicians had asked to play but as these last had gone away on tour, Swann could learn nothing further. He had a number of musical friends but, vividly as he could recall the pleasure the phrase had given him, and could see in his mind the forms it had traced, he was incapable of humming it to them and so, at last, he ceased to think of it.

But that night, at Mme Verdurin's, scarcely had the

young pianist begun to play than Swann sensed, stealing forth from beneath, murmuring, detached, the airy and perfumed phrase that he loved.   And it was so particularly itself, it had so individual a charm, that Swann felt as though he had met, in a friend's drawing room, a woman he had seen and admired in the street and had despaired of ever seeing again.   Finally the phrase receded, diligently guiding its successors, leaving on Swann's features the reflection of its smile. But now at last he could ask the name of his fair unknown and was told it was the andante of Vinteuil's sonata for piano and violin. He held it safe, could have it again to himself at home, as often as he wished, could study its language and acquire its secret.

And so, when the pianist had finished, Swann crossed the room and thanked him with a vivacity which delighted Mme Verdurin. "Isn't he a charmer?" she asked Swann, "doesn't he just understand his sonata, the little wretch?" The young pianist bowed, smiling and underlining each of his words: "You are most generous to me"

Swann began to tell Odette how he had fallen in love with that little phrase. When their hostess, who was some way off, called out "Well! It looks to me as though someone was saying nice things to you, Odette!" she replied "Yes, very nice" and he found her simplicity delightful. Then he asked for information about this Vinteuil: what else he had done, at what period in his life he had composed the sonata, and what meaning the little phrase could have had for him – that was what Swann wanted most to know. But none of these people who professed to admire this musician seemed ever to have asked himself these questions, for none of them was able to answer. Swann discovered no more than that the recent appearance of Vinteuil's sonata had caused a great stir among the school of musicians, but that it was unknown to the general public.

"I know someone called Vinteuil," said Swann, thinking of the old piano teacher at Combray.

"Perhaps he's the man" cried Mme Verdurin.

"Oh no, if you'd ever set eyes on him you wouldn't entertain the idea."

9

The little phrase continued to be associated in Swann's mind with Odette. He was well aware that his love was something that did not correspond to anything outside itself, he realized that Odette's qualities were not such as to justify his setting so high a value on the hours he spent in her company. And often, when the cold government of reason stood unchallenged in his mind, he would readily have ceased to sacrifice so many of his intellectual and social interests to this imaginary pleasure. But the little phrase had the power to liberate him; the proportions of Swann's soul were altered; Odette was purely individual, but assumed for him a sort of reality superior to that of concrete things. Thirst for an unknown delight was awakened in him by the little phrase, but without bringing him any precise gratification to assuage it. Those parts of Swann's soul which the little phrase had obliterated were left vacant by it, blank pages on which he was at liberty to inscribe the name of Odette. Moreover, in so far as Odette's affection might seem a little abrupt and disappointing, the little phrase would come to supplement it, to blend with its own mysterious essence. He would make Odette play it over to him again and again, ten, twenty times on end, insisting that as she did so she must never stop kissing him. "How do you expect me to play when you keep on holding me? I can't do everything at once. Make up your mind am I to play the phrase or play with you?" and he would get angry and she would burst out laughing, a laugh that was soon transformed and descended upon him in a shower of kisses.

He knew nothing of how she spent her time during the day, any more than of her past; so little, indeed that he had not even the tiny initial clue which, by allowing us to imagine what we do not know, stimulates a desire for knowledge. And so he never asked himself what she might be doing, or what her life had been. As a rule he met Odette only in the evenings; he was afraid of her growing tired of him if he visited her during the day as well but, being reluctant to forfeit the place that he held in her thoughts, he was constantly looking out for opportunities of claiming her attention. If, in a florist's or a jeweler's window, a plant or an ornament caught his eye, he would at once think of sending them to Odette, imagining the pleasure the sight of them had given him would be felt also by her, and would increase her affection for him. He was particularly anxious, always, that she should receive these presents before she went out for the evening, so her gratitude towards him might give additional tenderness to her welcome when he arrived at the Verdurins. He was pleased by this, as he was pleased by anything that might impress Odette with his love for her, or merely with his influence, with the extent to which he could be of use to her.

One evening it was pouring with rain and he had nothing but his Victoria. A friend offered to take him home in a closed carriage and he could have gone to bed with a quiet mind and an untroubled heart. But perhaps, if she saw that he seemed not to adhere to his resolution to spend the late evening always in her company, she might not bother to keep it free for him.

It was after eleven when he reached her door, and as he made his apology for having been unable to come away earlier, she complained that it was indeed very late, the storm had made her feel unwell, and she would not let him stay more than a half hour. A little while later she felt tired and wished to sleep. She asked him to put out the light before he went; he drew the curtains round her bed and left. But, when he was back in his own house, the idea struck him perhaps Odette was expecting someone, that the moment he had left the house she had opened her door to the man who was to spend the night with her. He went out, took a cab, and stopped it in a little street which lay at the back of her house and along which he used sometimes to go, to tap on her bedroom window, for her to let him in. Amid the glimmering blackness of the row of windows in which the lights had long since been put out, he saw one, and only one, from which percolated – between the slats of its shutters – a light which on other evenings had rejoiced his heart with its message: "She is there – expecting you" and now tortured him, saying: "She is there with the man she was expecting."

He must know who; he tiptoed along the wall but between the slanting bars he could see nothing, could only hear, in the silence of the night, the murmur of conversation. Certainly he suffered as he watched that light, in whose golden atmosphere, behind the closed sash, stirred the unseen and detested pair, the perfidy of Odette, and the pleasures she was enjoying with the stranger. And yet he was not sorry he had come, now that Odette's other life, of which he had a suspicion, was almost within his grasp. And perhaps the almost pleasurable sensation he felt at that moment was something more than the assuagement of a doubt, and of pain. If, since he had fallen in love, things had recovered a little of the delightful interest they had for him long ago – now it was another of the faculties of his studious youth that his jealousy revived; the passion for truth. At every other period in his life, the activities of another person had always seemed meaningless to Swann. But in this strange phase of love the personality of another person becomes so enlarged, so deepened, that the curiosity he now felt stirring inside him was the same thirst for knowledge with which he had once studied history. All manner of actions from which he would have recoiled in shame, such as spying outside a window, seemed to him now to be methods of scientific investigation with a genuine value and legitimately employable in the search for truth.

On the point of knocking on the shutters, he felt a pang of shame. She had often told him what a horror she had of jealous men. What he was about to do was singularly inept, and she would detest him for ever after, whereas for now, for the moment, for so long as he refrained from knocking, even in the act of infidelity, perhaps she loved him still. But his desire to know the truth was stronger, and seemed to him nobler. And moreover, the advantage which he felt that he had over them lay perhaps not so much in knowing as in being able to show them that he knew. He raised himself on tiptoe. He knocked. They had not heard; he knocked again, louder, and the conversation ceased. A man's voice – he strained to distinguish whose, asked:

"Who's there?"

He could not be certain of the voice. He knocked once again. The window first, then the shutters were thrown open. It was too late now to draw back, and he called out in a casual tone: "I wanted to know if you were feeling better."

Two old gentlemen stood facing him at the window, and beyond them he could see into a room he had never seen before. Having fallen into the habit, when he came late to Odette, of identifying her window by the fact it was the only one still lit up in a row of windows, he had been misled this time by the light, and had knocked at the window which belonged to the adjoining house. He made what apology he could and hurried home glad that, having feigned for so long a sort of indifference towards Odette, he had not now, by his jealousy, given her proof that he loved her too much which, between a pair of lovers, for ever dispenses the recipient from the obligation to love enough.

Physically, she was going through a bad phase; she was putting on weight, and the expressive charm of old seemed to have vanished with her first youth. He would gaze at her searchingly, trying to recapture the charm which he had once seen in her, and no longer finding it. Then he would look at photographs of her taken two years before and would remember how exquisite she had been. And that would console him a little for all the agony he suffered on her account.

When the Verdurins took her off to Saint-Germain he waited all night, to no purpose, for the Verdurins had decided to return early and Odette had been in Paris since midday. It had not occurred to her to tell him and not knowing what to do with herself she had spent the evening alone at a theatre, had long since gone home to bed, and was asleep. As a matter of fact, she had not even given him a thought. And such moments as these, in which she forgot Swann's very existence, were more useful to Odette, did more to bind him to her, than all her coquetry. For in this way Swann was kept in that state of painful agitation which had already been powerful enough to cause his love to blossom. There were times when he told himself that to allow so pretty a woman to go out by herself in Paris was as rash as to leave a case filled with jewels in the middle of the street. Although she would not allow him as a rule to meet her in public, saying that people would talk, it happened occasionally that, at an evening party to which he and she had both been invited – at Forcheville's, at the painter's, or at a charity ball – he found himself in the same room with her. He could see her but dared not stay for fear of annoying her by spying upon the pleasures she enjoyed in other company, pleasures which – as he drove home in utter loneliness and went to bed miserable as I was to be some years later on the evenings when he came to dine with us at Combray – seemed to him limitless since he had not seen the end of them.

At times, he would imagine that Odette was Forcheville's mistress. At such times Swann detested her. "But I've been a fool, too" he would argue. "I'm paying for other men's pleasures with my money. All the same, she'd better take care, and not push her luck, because I might very well stop giving her anything at all." And his hatred, like his love, needing to manifest itself in action, he took pleasure in urging his evil imaginings further and further. Certainly, of the extent of this love Swann had no direct awareness. When he sought to measure it, it happened sometimes that he found it diminished, shrunk almost to nothing; for instance, the lack of enthusiasm, amounting almost to distaste, which, in the days before he was in love with Odette, he had felt for her features returned on certain days. "Really, I'm making distinct headway" he would tell himself next day. "Looking at things quite honestly, I can't say I got much pleasure last night from being in bed with her." And certainly he was sincere, but his love extended a long way beyond the province of physical desire. My uncle advised Swann not to see Odette for some days, after which she would love him all the more. A few days later Odette told Swann she had just had a rude awakening, on discovering that my uncle was the same as other men: he had tried to take her by force. She calmed Swann down when he wanted to challenge my uncle to a duel, but he refused to shake hands with him when they met again. And yet he would have liked to live until the time came when he no longer loved her, when she would have no reason for lying to him. Often for several days on end the suspicion that she was in love with someone else would distract his mind from the question of Forcheville, making it almost immaterial to him, like those new developments in a continuous state of ill-health which seem momentarily to have delivered us. There were even days when he was not tormented by suspicion. He fancied that he was cured. But his meticulous prudence was defeated one evening when he had gone out to a party.

It was at the Marquise de Saint-Euverte's, the last for that season of the evenings on which she invited people to listen to the musicians who would serve, later on, for her charity concerts. Swann had gone forward into the room at Mme de Saint-Euverte's insistence, and in order to listen to an air from Orfeo which was being rendered on the flute, had taken up a position in a corner from which, unfortunately, his horizon was bounded by two ladies of mature years seated side by side, the Marquise de Cambremer and the Vicomtesse de Franquetot who, because they were cousins, spent their time at parties wandering through the room hunting for one another like people at a railway station, and could never be at rest until they had reserved two adjacent chairs by marking them with their fans or handkerchiefs.

The pianist having finished the Liszt intermezzo and begun a prelude by Chopin, Mme de Cambremer turned to Mme de Franquetot with a fond smile of knowing satisfaction and allusion to the past. She had learned in her girlhood to fondle and cherish those long sinuous phrases of Chopin, so free, so flexible, so tactile, which begin by reaching out and exploring far outside and away from the direction in which they started, far beyond the point which one might have expected their notes to reach, and which divert themselves in those byways of fantasy only to return more deliberately — with a premeditated reprise, with more precision, as on a crystal bowl that reverberates - to strike at your heart.

Swann wanted to go home, but just as he was making his escape, General de Froberville caught him and asked for an introduction to Mme de Cambremer, and he was obliged to go back into the room to look for her.

"I say, Swann, I'd rather be married to that little woman than slaughtered by savages, what do you say?"
The words "slaughtered by savages" pierced Swann's aching heart; and at once he felt the need to continue the conversation. "Ah!" he began "some fine lives have been lost in that way...there was, you remember, that navigator, La Perouse..." and he was at once happy again. "He was a fine character, and interests me very much"

"Oh yes, of course, La Perouse" said the General "There's a street called that."

"Do you know anyone in the Rue La Perouse?" asked Swann excitedly.

"Only Mme de Chanlivault, the sister of that good fellow Chaussepierre. She gave a most amusing theatre-party the other evening"

When Swann did finally introduce de Froberville to the young Mme de Cambremer, the concert had begun again and Swann saw that he could not now go before the end of the new number. He suffered greatly from being shut up among all these people since, being ignorant of his love, they made it a subjective state which existed for himself alone, whose reality there was nothing external to confirm. He suffered above all from having to prolong his exile in this place to which Odette would never come, from which she was entirely absent.

But suddenly it was as though she had entered, and his hand clutched at his heart. The violin had risen to a series of high notes on which it rested as though awaiting something, in the exaltation of seeing the object of its expectation approaching, and with a desperate effort to last until its arrival, as one holds a door open. And before Swann had time to understand and say to himself "It's the little phrase from Vinteuil's sonata – I mustn't listen!" all his memories of the days when Odette had been in love, which he had succeeded until that moment in keeping invisible in the depths of his being, deceived by this sudden reflection of a season of love whose sun, they supposed, had dawned again, had awakened from their slumber, had taken wing and risen to sing maddeningly in his ears, without pity for his desolation, the forgotten strains of happiness.

There are in the music of the violin, accents so akin to those of certain voices that one has the illusion a singer has taken her place amid the orchestra. One raises one's eyes and sees only the wooden case, but at times thinks one is listening to a captive genie struggling in the darkness of the quivering box. Sometimes it is in the air, at large, like a pure and supernatural being that unfolds its invisible message as it goes by.

Swann, who experienced something like the refreshing sense of a metamorphosis in the momentary blindness with which he was struck as he approached it, felt its presence like that of a protective goddess, a confidante of his love who, in order to come to him through the crowd and draw him aside to speak to him, had disguised herself in this sweeping cloak of sound. And as she passed, telling him what she had to say, he made with his lips the motion of kissing. He felt he was no longer in exile and alone since she, who addressed herself to him, was whispering to him of Odette. For he had no longer, as of old, the impression that Odette and he were unknown to the little phrase. Had it not been the witness of their joys? True that, as often, it had warned him of their frailty. And of those sorrows which the little phrase foreshadowed to him then, it seemed to say to him "what does it all matter? It means nothing." And Swann's thoughts were borne for the first time on a wave of tenderness towards Vinteuil, who must also have suffered so greatly. From the depths of what well of sorrow could he have drawn that unlimited power of creation?

The phrase had disappeared. Swann knew that it would come again at the end of the last movement. And his personality was now so divided that the strain of waiting for the moment when he would find himself face to face with it again shook him with one of those sobs a beautiful line of poetry or a sad piece of news will wring from us, not when we are alone, but when we impart them to friends in whom we see ourselves reflected. It reappeared, but this time to remain poised in the air, to sport there for a moment only, as though immobile, and shortly to expire. And so Swann lost nothing of the previous time for which it lingered. It was still there, like a bubble that floats for a while unbroken. As a rainbow seems to subside, then soars again with greater splendor; so to the two colours which the little phrase had hitherto allowed to appear it added others now, chords shot with every hue in the prism. Swann dared not move, and would have liked to compel all the other people in the room to remain still also, as if the slightest movement might imperil the presence that was so soon to vanish. But no one, as it happened, dreamed of speaking. When the phrase unraveled itself at last, and only its echoes floated among the subsequent themes, Swann understood that the feeling which Odette had once had for him would never revive, that his hopes of happiness would not be realised now. If he had been living at a distance from Odette he would gradually have lost interest in her. He would have been glad to learn that she was leaving Paris for ever; he would have had the heart to remain there, but he hadn't the heart to go.

10

Among the rooms which used most commonly to take shape in my mind during my nights of sleeplessness, there was none that differed more utterly from the rooms at Combray, thickly powdered with the motes of an atmosphere granular, pollinated, edible and devout, than my room in the Grand Hotel de la Plage, at Balbec, the walls of which enclosed a finer air, pure, azure-tinted, saline. The Bavarian entrusted with furnishing this hotel had set against the walls, on three sides, a series of low book-cases with glass fronts, in which was reflected this or that section of the view, so that the walls were lined with sea-scapes, interrupted only by the polished mahogany of the actual shelves. And yet nothing could have differed more from the real Balbec than that other Balbec of which I often dreamed, on stormy days, when the wind was so strong that Francoise, as she took me to the Champs-Elysees, would advise me not to walk too close to the walls or I might have my head knocked off by a falling slate. I longed for nothing more than to behold a stormy sea, less as a mighty spectacle than as a momentary revelation of the true life of nature. I required also, if the storm was to be absolutely genuine, that the shore from which I watched it should be a natural shore, not an embankment constructed by a municipality.

If my health had grown stronger and my parents allowed me, if not to actually go down to stay at Balbec, at least to take, just once, in order to become acquainted with the architecture and landscapes of Normandy or of Brittany, that train into which I had so often clambered in imagination, I should have wished to stop at the most beautiful of its towns; but in vain did I compare and contrast them. My parents had to be content with sending me every day to the Champs-Elysees, in the custody of a person who would see that I did not tire myself; this person being none other than Francoise, who had entered our service after the death of my aunt Leonie. Going to the Champs-Elysees I found unendurable. If only Bergotte had described the place in one of his books, I should no doubt have longed to get to know it, like so many things of which a simulacrum had first found its way into my imagination. This breathed life into them, gave them a personality, and I sought then to rediscover them in reality; but in this public garden there was nothing that attached itself to my dreams.

One day, as I was bored with our usual place beside the roundabout, Francoise had taken me for an excursion into neighboring regions, then gone back to collect things from her chair. While I waited for her I was pacing the broad lawn dominated, at its far end, by a statue rising from a fountain, in front of which a little girl with reddish hair was playing battledore and shuttlecock, when from the path another little girl, who was putting on her coat and covering up her racquet, called out sharply: "Goodbye Gilberte, I'm going home now; don't forget we're coming to you this evening, after dinner." The name passed close by me, evoking forcefully the girl whom it labeled - Mlle Swann - who continued to launch and retrieve her shuttlecock until a governess with a blue feather in her hat called her away.

Next day she was not there; but I saw her on the following days, and spent all my time revolving round the spot where she played with her friends, to such effect that once, when they found there were not enough of them to make up a prisoner's base, she sent one to ask me if I cared to complete their side, and from that day I played with her whenever she came. But this did not happen every day; there were days when she was prevented from coming by the whole of that life, separated from my own, which I had felt pass close to me, in the hawthorn lane near Combray and on the grass of the Champs-Elysees. On such days she would tell us in advance we would not be seeing her; if it was because of her lessons she would say: "It's too tiresome, I shan't be able to come tomorrow; you'll all be enjoying yourselves here without me," with an air of regret which to some extent consoled me; If, on the other hand, she had been invited to a party, and I asked her whether she was coming, she would reply: "I should hope not! I hope Mamma will let me go to my friend's." But on these days I did at least know I would not see her, whereas on others, without any warning, her mother would take her shopping, and next day she would say: "Oh, yes! I went out" as though it had been the most natural thing in the

78

world, and not the greatest possible misfortune for someone else.

There were also days of bad weather on which her governess, afraid on her own account of the rain, would not bring Gilberte. And on those days when all other vegetation had disappeared, when the fine green hide which covered the trunks of old trees was hidden beneath the snow, we found no one, or only a solitary little girl on the point of departure, who assured me Gilberte was not coming. The chairs, deserted by shivering governesses, stood empty. Francoise found it too cold to stand about, so we walked to the Pont de la Concorde to see the Seine frozen over.

Suddenly the sky was rent in two; between the Punch-and Judy and the horses, against the opening horizon, I had just seen Mademoiselle's blue feather. And now Gilberte was running at full speed towards me, sparkling and rosy beneath a cap trimmed with fur. Shortly before she reached me she slid along the ice and, either to keep her balance, or because it appeared graceful, or else pretending that she was on skates, it was with outstretched arms she advanced, to embrace me. "You are like me, faithful at all costs to our old Champs-Elysees. We're two brave souls!"

The first of these days - to which the snow, a symbol of the powers that could deprive me of the sight of Gilberte, imparted the sadness of a day of separation, that day none the less marked a stage in the progress of my love, for it was like a first sorrow we shared together. There were only our two selves of our little company, and to be alone with her was not merely like a beginning of intimacy, but also-as though she had come there solely to please me in such weather- it seemed to me as touching as if, on one of those days when she had been invited to a party, she had given it up in order to come join me. This day which I had so dreaded was, as it happened, one of the few on which I was not unduly wretched.

That complexity came to me again this year, on one of those mornings early in November when, in Paris, if we stay indoors, being so near and yet excluded from the transformation of Autumn, which is drawing to a close, we feel a veritable fever of yearning for the fallen leaves. And on that morning, no longer hearing the splash of rain as on preceding days, seeing the smile of fine weather at the corners of my drawn curtains, as at the corners of closed lips betraying the secret of happiness, I had felt I might be able to look at those yellow leaves with the light shining through them; and being no more able to restrain myself from going to see the trees than, in my childhood days I had been able to resist the longing to visit the sea, I had risen and left the house.

The idea of perfection I had within me I had bestowed, in that other time, upon the height of a victoria, upon the raking thinness of horses, frenzied and light as wasps on the wing. Alas! There was nothing now but motor-cars driven each by a moustached mechanic. I wished to hold before my eyes, to see whether they were indeed as charming as they appeared to memory, little women's hats, so low crowned as to seem no more than garlands. All the hats now were immense, covered with fruits and flowers and birds. On the heads of gentlemen

I no longer found the grey "toppers" of old, nor indeed any other kind; they went out bare-headed. And seeing all these new components of the spectacle, I had no longer a belief to infuse into them; they passed before me in a meaningless fashion, containing in themselves no beauty. They were just women, in whose elegance I had no faith. When a belief vanishes, there survives it-more and more vigorously so as to cloak the absence of the power, now lost to us, of imparting reality to new things-a fetishistic attachment to the old things which it did once animate, as if it was in them and not in ourselves the divine spark resided.

The sun had gone. The wind wrinkled the surface of the Lac, and seemed to proclaim inhuman emptiness, and helped me to understand how paradoxical it is to seek in reality the pictures stored in one's memory, which lose the charm that comes from the senses. The reality I had known no longer existed. The places we have known do not belong to the world of space on which we map them. They were only a thin slice, held between impressions that composed our life at that time; the memory of a particular image is but regret for a particular moment; and houses, roads, avenues are as fugitive as the years.

11 - IN THE SHADOW OF YOUNG GIRLS IN FLOWER

My mother, when it was a question of having M de Norpois to dinner for the first time, having expressed her regret that Professor Cottard was away and that she had quite ceased to see anything of Swann, since either of these might have helped to entertain the ex-ambassador, my father replied that Swann was a vulgar show-off whom the Marquis de Norpois would be sure to dismiss. Now this attitude on my father's part may require a few words of explanation inasmuch as some of us no doubt remember a Swann by whom modesty and discretion in all his social relations were carried to the utmost refinement of delicacy. But what had happened was that, to the original "young Swann" and also to the Swann of the Jockey Club, our old friend had added a new personality (which was not to be his last), that of Odette's husband. Adapting to the humble ambitions of that lady the instinct, the desire, the industry which he had always had, he laboriously constructed for himself, a long way beneath the old, a new position more appropriate to the companion who was to share it with him.

The evening on which M de Norpois first appeared at our table, in a year when I still went to play in the Champs-Elysees, has remained fixed in my memory because the afternoon of the same day I at last went to a matinee to see Berma in *Phedre,* and also because in talking to M de Norpois I realised suddenly how completely the feelings aroused in me by Gilberte Swann and her parents differed from those which the same family inspired in everyone else. I was introduced to him before dinner by my father, who summoned me into his study for the purpose. As I entered, the Ambassador rose, held out his hand, bowed his tall figure and fixed his blue eyes attentively on my face. As the foreign visitors who used to be presented to him were all persons of note, with regard to whom he knew he would be able to say later on, when he heard their names mentioned in Paris or in Petersburg, that he remembered perfectly the evening he spent with them in Munich or Sofia, he had formed the habit of impressing upon them the pleasure he felt in making their acquaintance. He put a number of questions to me about my life and my studies, and about my tastes which I heard spoken of for the first time as though it might be a reasonable thing to obey their promptings. Since they inclined me towards literature, he did not dissuade me; on the contrary he spoke with deference, as of some charming person in Rome one remembers with pleasure and regrets one's duties enable one to revisit so seldom. He appeared to envy me the delightful hours which, more fortunate than himself and more free, I should be able to spend with such a mistress.

My Aunt Leonie had bequeathed to me, together with a multiplicity of objects and furniture, almost all her liquid assets - revealing after her death an affection I had little suspected in her lifetime. My father, who was trustee of this estate until I came of age, now consulted M de Norpois with regard to a number of investments. M de Norpois gave a just perceptible smile of congratulation; like all capitalists, he regarded wealth as an enviable thing, but thought it more delicate to compliment people upon their possessions only by an inconspicuous sign of intelligent sympathy; at the same time, as he was himself colossally rich, he thought it in good taste to seem to regard as considerable the inferior income of his friends with, however, a happy and comforting reference to the superiority of his own.

"Tell me, were you at the Foreign Ministry dinner last night?" asked my father "I couldn't go."

"No" M de Norpois smiled, "I must confess I renounced it for a party of a very different sort. I was dining with the beautiful Mme Swann."

"Was there a writer of the name Bergotte at this dinner, Monsieur?" I asked timidly, trying to keep the conversation to the subject of the Swanns.

"Yes, Bergotte was there" replied M de Norpois,

inclining his head courteously towards me, "Do you know him?"

"My son does not know him but admires his work immensely," my mother explained.

"And was Mme Swann's daughter at the dinner?" I asked, taking advantage of a moment in which, as we all moved towards the drawing room, I could more easily conceal my emotion.   M de Norpois appeared to be trying to remember:

"Ah, yes, a young person of fourteen or fifteen? Yes, I remember now she was introduced to me before dinner as the daughter. I'm afraid I saw little of her, she retired early or else went out to see friends - I forget which. But I can see you are intimate with the household."

"I play with Mlle Swann in the Champs-Elysees, and she's delightful."

"Oh! So that's it? But I assure you, I too thought her charming. I must confess to you, however, that I do not believe she will ever come near her mother, if I may say as much without hurting your feelings."

"I admire her mother, too, enormously."

"Ah! I must tell them; they will be flattered."

After M de Norpois had gone my mother appeared none too pleased that my father no longer thought of a diplomatic career for me. I fancy that, anxious above all else that a definite rule of life should discipline the vagaries of my nervous system, what she regretted was not so much seeing me abandon diplomacy as the prospect of my devoting myself to literature. "Don't worry," my father told her, "the main thing is that a man should find pleasure in his work. He's no longer a child. He knows pretty well now what he likes, it's very unlikely that he will change, and he's quite capable of deciding for himself what will make him happy."

12

I continued to go to the Champs-Elysees on fine days, along streets whose elegant pink houses seemed to be washed (because exhibitions of watercolors were then the height of fashion) in a lightly floating atmosphere. For some time past, in certain households, the name of the Champs-Elysees would be greeted by the mothers with that baleful air which they reserve for a physician of established reputation whom they have seen make too many false diagnoses; people insisted these gardens were not good for children, that they knew of more than one case of measles and any number of feverish chills for which they must be held responsible. There was talk of my no longer being allowed to go, but I felt sure this was only a pretext so I should no longer be able to see Mlle Swann, and I forced myself to repeat the name of Gilberte all the time.

Sometimes my mother would stroke my forehead, saying "So little boys don't tell Mamma their troubles any more?" And Francoise used to come up to me every day and say: "What a face, to be sure! If you could just see yourself!"

One day, after the postman called, my mother laid a letter upon my bed. I opened it carelessly, since it could not bear the one signature that would have made me happy, the name of Gilberte, with whom I had no relations outside the Champs-Elysees. But there, at the foot of the page, which was embossed with a silver seal representing a helmeted head, was precisely Gilberte's signature. "My dear friend," said the letter, "I hear you have been ill and have given up going to the Champs. I hardly ever go there either because there has been such an enormous lot of illness. But my friends come to tea here every Monday and Friday. Mamma asks me to tell you that it will be a great pleasure to us all if you will come too as soon as you are well. Good by, my friend, with all my kindest regards. G I L B E R T E"

Life is strewn with these miracles for which people who love can always hope. It is possible this one had been brought about by my mother who, seeing that I had lost all interest in life, may have suggested to Gilberte to write to me just as, when I first went sea bathing, in order to make me enjoy diving which I hated, she used secretly to hand my bathing instructor marvelous boxes made of shells and branches of coral which I believed I myself discovered lying at the bottom of the sea. With love, it is best to make no attempt to understand. The same mystery which veils from our eyes the reason for a catastrophe envelops just as frequently, when love is in question, the suddenness of certain happy solutions.

Thus at length I came to know that house from which was wafted even on to the staircase the scent Mme Swann used, but which was more redolent still of the peculiar, disturbing charm of Gilberte. On the days when I was to go out with the Swanns I would arrive at their house in time for lunch. As one was not expected before half past twelve, while my parents in those days had their meal at a quarter past eleven, it was not until they had risen from table that I made my way. On frosty days in winter if the weather was fine, looking to see that my patent-leather boots were not getting dirty, I would wander up and down the avenues, waiting until twenty-seven minutes past the hour. At this hour when ordinarily I did not notice them, I seemed now to be discovering the fine weather, the cold, the wintry sunlight, it was all as a sort of preface to the habitation of Mme Swann, in the heart of which there was by contrast so much warmth, so many scents and flowers.

A favor still more precious than their taking me with them to the zoo or a concert, the Swanns did not exclude me even from their friendship with Bergotte, which had been at the root of the attraction I had found in them when, before I had even seen Gilberte, I reflected that her intimacy with that godlike elder would have made her, for me, the most enthralling of friends. One day, Mme Swann invited me to a big luncheon party. There were sixteen people among whom I never suspected for a moment that I was to find Bergotte. Mme Swann, who had already named me to several of her guests, suddenly, after my name, pronounced that of the gentle Bard. The name Bergotte made me start, like the sound of a revolver. There, in front of me, was a youngish, uncouth, thickset and myopic little man, with a red nose curled like a snail shell and a goatee beard. I was cruelly disappointed, for what had just vanished was the beauty of an immense work which I had contrived to enshrine in the frail and hallowed organism that I had constructed, like a temple, expressly for it, but for which no room was to be found in the squat figure of the little man with the snub nose and black beard who stood before me. The whole of the Bergotte whom I had elaborated for myself out of the beauty of his books ceased to be of any possible use the moment I was obliged to include in him the nose and the beard - just as we must reject as worthless the solution we have found for a problem the terms of which we had not read in full and so failed to observe that the total must amount to a specified figure.

Meanwhile we had taken our places at table. Bergotte was sitting not far from me and I could hear quite clearly everything that he said. It was a long time before I discovered an exact correspondence with his books, in which his form became so poetic and so musical. Bergotte appeared almost to be talking nonsense, intoning certain words and, pursuing beneath them a single image, stringing them together with a wearisome monotony. The quality of what he wrote was expressed in conversation by so subtle a manner of approaching a question, ignoring every aspect of it that was already familiar, that he appeared to be seizing hold of an unimportant detail, to be off the point, so that his ideas seemed as often as not to be confused, for each of us sees clarity only in those ideas which have the same degree of confusion as his own. Besides, as novelty depends upon the elimination of the attitude to which we had grown accustomed, any new form of conversation - like all original painting and music - must always appear complicated and exhausting.

Certain peculiarities of elocution, faint traces of which were to be found in Bergotte's conversation, were not exclusively his own; for when, later on, I came to know his brothers and sisters I found those much more pronounced in them. There was something abrupt and harsh in the closing words of a cheerful sentence, something faint and dying at the end of a sad one. Swann, who had known the Master as a boy, told me that in those days one used to hear on his lips, just as much as on his brothers' and sisters', those family inflexions, shouts of violent merriment interspersed with murmurings of a long drawn melancholy, and that in the room in which they all played together he used to perform his part better than any of them, alternately deafening and subdued. But, from the moment when he transferred them to his books, he ceased to make use of them in his speech. From the day on which he had begun to write his voice had abandoned this orchestration for ever.

If, however, despite all the similarities I was to perceive between the writer and the man, I had not at first sight believed this could be Bergotte, perhaps I was not altogether wrong, for he himself did not, in the strict sense of the word, believe it either. He did not believe it since he showed some alacrity in ingratiating himself with fashionable people and with literary men and journalists who were vastly inferior. He had long since learned he had genius, compared to which social position and official rank were nothing. But he continued to simulate deference towards mediocre writers in order to succeed in becoming an Academician. And the man with the beard and nose knew and used all the tricks in his efforts to reach the coveted academic chair. One could hear, alternating with the speech of the true Bergotte, that of the selfish and ambitious Bergotte who talked only of his powerful, rich or noble friends in order to enhance himself - he who in his books, when he was really himself, had so well portrayed the charm of the poor.

Above all, he was a man who in his heart of hearts only really loved images and painting them in words. For a trifle someone had sent him, if that trifle gave him the opportunity of weaving a few images round it, he would be prodigal in the expression of his gratitude, while showing none whatever for an expensive present. That first day I met him with Gilberte's parents, I mentioned to Bergotte I had recently been to see Berma in *Phedre,* and he told me that in the scene in which she stood with her arm raised to her shoulders she had managed to suggest certain classical figures, a Hesperid at Olympia, and also the primitive virgins on the Erechtheum.

I let myself go in telling him what my impressions had been. Often Bergotte disagreed but he allowed me to go on talking. I told him I liked the green light which was turned on when Phedre raised her arm "Ah! The designer will be glad to hear that; he's a real artist and I shall tell him you liked it, because he is very proud of that effect. I must say, myself, that I don't care for it much, it bathes everything in a sort of glow, little Phedre standing there looks too like a branch of coral on the floor of an aquarium. You will tell me, of course, that it brings out the cosmic aspect of the play. That's quite true. All the same, it would be more appropriate if the scene were laid in the Court of Neptune. Still, it's what my friend wanted, and it's very well done, right or wrong, and really quite pretty. Yes, so you liked it, did you; you understood what he was after. We feel the same about it, don't we, really: it's a bit crazy, what he's done, you agree with me, but on the whole it's very clever." And when Bergotte's opinion was contrary to mine, he in no way reduced me to silence, as M de Norpois would have done. Just as priests are best able to pardon the sins they do not themselves commit, so genius can best understand the ideas most directly in opposition to its own.

I ought to have told myself all this, but I did not; I was convinced that I had appeared a fool to Bergotte, when Gilberte whispered in my ear: "You can't think how overjoyed I am, because you've made a conquest of my great friend. He's been telling Mamma he found you extremely intelligent."

As Bergotte lived in the same neighborhood as my parents, we left the house together. In the carriage he spoke to me of my health: "Our friends were telling me you had been ill. I'm sorry. And yet, not too sorry, because I can see quite well that you are able to enjoy the pleasures of the mind, and they are what means most."

He did not convince me, of course, and yet I already felt happier, less constricted. I had regarded my moments of day-dreaming, of enthusiasm, of self-confidence as purely subjective and false. But according to Bergotte, who appeared to understand my case, it seemed that it was quite the contrary, that the symptom I ought to disregard was, in fact, my doubts.

"I should recommend you" went on Bergotte, "to consult Dr du Boulbon, who is an extremely intelligent man." "He's a great admirer of your books" I replied. I saw that Bergotte knew this, and I concluded that kindred spirits soon come together.

"I'll tell you who does need a good doctor, and that's our friend Swann," said Bergotte. And on my asking whether he was ill, "Well, don't you see, he's typical of the man who has married a whore, and has to pocket a dozen insults a day from women who refuse to meet his wife or men who have slept with her. Just look, one day when you're there, at the way he lifts his eyebrows when he comes in, to see who's in the room."

The malice with which Bergotte spoke thus to a stranger of the friends in whose house he had for so long been received as a welcome guest was as new to me as the tender tone he adopted in their presence.

My parents meanwhile would have liked to see the intelligence Bergotte had discerned in me manifest in some piece of work. When I still did not know the Swanns I thought I was prevented from working by the impossibility of seeing Gilberte. But now their door stood open to me, scarcely had I sat down at my desk I would get up and hurry round to them. To my parents it seemed almost as though, idle as I was, I was leading, since it was spent in the same salon as a great writer, the life most favourable to the growth of talent. The person, incidentally, who was most completely taken in by this illusion was Mme Swann.

Thus, no more from the Swanns than from my parents, was there any further opposition to that existence in which I might see Gilberte as often as I chose, with enchantment if not with peace of mind. There can be no peace of mind in love, since what one has obtained is never anything but a new starting-point for further desires. So long as I had been unable to go to her house, with my eyes fixed on that inaccessible happiness, I could not even imagine the fresh grounds for anxiety that lay in wait for me there. But at least I was happy, and no further threat arose to endanger my happiness.

One was to appear, alas, from a quarter in which I had never detected any peril, namely from Gilberte and myself. I should have been tormented by what reassured me. We are, when we love, in an abnormal state, capable of giving at once to the most apparently simple accident, a seriousness which in itself it would not entail. What makes us so happy is the presence in our hearts of an unstable element which we contrive perpetually to maintain and of which we cease almost to be aware so long as it is not displaced. In reality, there is in love a permanent strain of suffering which happiness neutralises, makes potential, postpones, but which may at any moment become excruciating.

On several occasions I sensed that Gilberte was anxious to put off my visits. It is true that when I was at all anxious to see her I had only to get myself invited by her parents who were increasingly persuaded of my excellent influence. "Thanks to them" I thought, "my love is in no danger; seeing that I have them on my side, I can set my mind at rest since they have complete authority over Gilberte." Until, detecting signs of impatience which she betrayed when her father asked me to the house, I wondered whether what I had regarded as a protection for my happiness was not in fact the reason that happiness could not last.

13

I had arrived at a state of almost complete indifference to Gilberte when, two years later, I went with my grandmother to Balbec. When I succumbed to the attraction of a new face, I said to myself sadly that this love of ours, in so far as it is a love for one particular creature, is not perhaps a very real thing, since though associations of pleasant or painful musings can attach it for a time to a woman to the extent of making us believe it has been inspired by her, if on the other hand we detach ourselves deliberately from those associations this love, as though it were in fact spontaneous and sprang from ourselves alone, will revive in order to bestow itself on another woman. At the time, however, of my departure for Balbec, and during the earlier part of my stay there, my indifference was still only intermittent. Often, our life being so careless of chronology, interpolating so many anachronisms into the sequence of our days, I found myself living in those far older days than yesterday or last week when I still loved Gilberte. And then no longer seeing her became suddenly painful, as it would have been at that time. The self that had loved her would reappear, stimulated far more often by a trivial than by an important event.

For instance, I heard someone who passed me on the seafront at Balbec refer to "the head of the Ministry of Posts and his family." Now, since I as yet knew nothing of the influence that family was to have on my life, this remark ought to have passed unheeded; instead it gave me an acute twinge, which a self, that had for the most part long since been outgrown, felt at being parted from Gilberte. For I had never given another thought to a conversation which Gilberte had had with her father in my hearing, in which allusion was made to the Secretary to the Ministry of Posts and his family. Now the memories of love are no exception to the general laws of memory, which in turn are governed by the still more general laws of Habit. And as Habit weakens everything, what best reminds us of a person is precisely what we had forgotten (because it was of no importance, and we therefore left it in full possession of its strength). That is why the better part of our memories exists outside us, in a blatter of rain, in the smell of an unaired room or of the first crackling brushwood fire in a cold grate: Wherever, in short, we happen upon what our mind, having no use for it, had rejected; the last treasure the past has in store. Within us but hidden in oblivion, it is thanks to this oblivion that we can from time to time recover the person that we were. In the broad daylight of habitual memory the past turns gradually pale and fades out of sight, we shall never recapture it. Or rather we should never recapture it had not a few words (such as "head of the Ministry of Posts") been carefully locked away, as an author deposits in the National Library a book which might otherwise become unobtainable.

But this recrudescence of my love for Gilberte lasted no longer than such things last in a dream, and my sense of loneliness was further increased a moment later. When I confessed to my grandmother that I did not feel well, that I thought we should return to Paris, she had offered no protest, saying merely that she was going out to buy a few things which would be equally useful whether we left or stayed. While I waited for her, I had taken a turn through the streets, which were packed with a crowd of people. The need I now felt for my grandmother was enhanced by fear I had shattered another of her illusions. She must be feeling discouraged, feeling that if I could not stand the fatigue of this journey there was no hope that any change of air could ever do me good. I decided to return to the hotel and lie down for a little while on the bed.

It is our noticing them that puts things in a room, our growing used to them that takes them away again and clears a space for us. Space there was none in my bedroom at Balbec; it was full of things which did not know me, which flung back at me the distrustful glance I cast at them, and without taking any heed of my existence, showed that I was interrupting the humdrum course of theirs. Having no world, no room, penetrated to the very bones by fever, I was alone and longed to die. Then my grandmother came in and to the expansion of my constricted heart there opened at once an infinity of space.

She was wearing a loose cambric dressing gown which she put on at home whenever any of us was ill and which was her servant's smock, her nurse's uniform, her nun's habit. Like a man who tries to fasten his tie in front of a glass and forgets that the end which he sees reflected is not on the side to which he raises his hand, or like a dog that chases the shadow of an insect, I threw myself into the arms of my grandmother and pressed my lips to her face as though I were thus gaining access to that immense heart she opened to me.

Afterwards, I gazed inexhaustibly at her large face, outlined like a cloud, glowing and serene, behind which I could discern the radiance of her tender love. With outstretched hands I smoothed her beautiful hair, still hardly grey, with as much respect and gentleness as if I had actually been caressing her goodness. She found such pleasure in taking any trouble that saved me one that when, having seen that she wished to help me undress and go to bed, I made as though to stop her and to undress myself, with an imploring gaze she arrested my hands as they fumbled with the top buttons of my jacket and my boots.

"Oh, do let me!" she begged "It's such a joy for your Granny. And be sure you knock on the wall if you want anything in the night. My bed is just on the other side, and the partition is quite thin. Just give a knock now, as soon as you're in bed, so that we shall know where we are.

And sure enough that evening I gave three knocks, and scarcely had I given my taps than I heard three others, in a different tone from mine, stamped with a calm authority, repeated twice over so there should be no mistake, and saying to me plainly: "Don't get agitated; I've heard you", a sweet moment which opened like a symphony with the rhythmical dialogue of my three taps, to which the wall of my bedroom, steeped in love and joy, responded.

14

On this first night after our arrival, when my grandmother had left me, I began again to suffer as I had suffered the day before, in Paris, at the moment of leaving home. But next morning! - while I was washing and dressing myself and trying in vain to find things in my trunk, from which I extracted, pell-mell, only a lot of things of no use, what a joy it was, thinking already of the pleasure of lunch and a walk along the shore, to see in the window, and in all the glass fronts of the bookcases, as in the portholes of a ship's cabin, the open sea, and to follow with my eyes the waves that leapt up one another like jumpers on a trampoline. Every other moment, holding the starched towel with the name of the hotel upon it, with which I was making futile efforts to dry myself, I returned to the window to have another look at that vast, dazzling, mountainous ampitheatre, and at the snowy crests of its emerald waves.

Chance put into our hands, my grandmother's and mine, the means of acquiring instantaneous prestige in the eyes of the other occupants of the hotel. For on that first afternoon at the moment when the lady came downstairs from her room, producing, thanks to the footman who preceded her and the maid who came running after her with a book and a rug she had forgotten, a marked effect upon all who beheld her and arousing in each of them a curiosity from which it was evident that none was immune, the manager leaned across to my grandmother and out of kindness whispered in her ear "The Marquise de Villeparisis!" at the same moment the old lady, catching sight of my grandmother, could not repress a start of pleased surprise. If there was one person who, more than anyone else, lived shut up in a world of her own, it was my grandmother. I dared not confess to her that if people had seen her talking to Mme de Villeparisis, I should have been immensely gratified, because the Marquise enjoyed some prestige in the hotel and her friendship would have given us status. It must be added that no one else took the trouble to be so continually nice to us. Whenever my grandmother remarked on a book that Mme de Villeparisis was reading, or said she had been admiring the fruit which someone had just sent to our friend, within an hour the footman would come to our rooms with book or fruit.

A few days later we met Mme de Villeparisis as we came away from the symphony concert and, on our way back to the hotel, had stopped for a moment on the front. "Are you," she asked me, "the son of the Permanent Secretary at the Ministry? Indeed! I'm told your father is a most charming man." My grandmother bade Mme Villeparisis goodbye, so that we might stay and imbibe the fresh air for a little while longer outside the hotel, until they signaled to us that our lunch was ready. But the Balbec doctor, called in to cope with a sudden feverish attack, gave the opinion that I ought not to stay out all day in the sun during the hot weather, and wrote out various prescriptions for me. My grandmother took these in a show of respect in which I could determine her resolve to ignore them, but did pay attention to the advice on the question of hygiene, and accepted an offer from Mme de Villeparisis to take us for drives in her carriage.

We would set off; sometime after rounding the railway station we came into a country road which soon became as familiar to me as the roads round Combray, from the bend where it took off between charming orchards to the turning at which we left it where there were tilled fields on either side. Among these we could see here and there an apple tree, stripped true of its blossoms and bearing no more than a fringe of pistils but sufficient even so to enchant me since I could imagine, seeing those leaves, how their broad expanse, like the ceremonial carpet spread for a wedding that was now over, had been only recently swept by the white satin train of their blushing flowers.

Mme de Villeparisis, seeing that I was fond of churches, promised me that we should visit several of them, and especially the church at Carqueville "quite buried in all its old ivy" as she said with a gesture of her hand which seemed tastefully to be clothing the absent facade in an invisible and delicate screen of foliage.

Sometimes, as the carriage laboured up a steep road through ploughlands a few hesitant cornflowers, like those of Combray, would follow in our wake. Presently the horses outdistanced them, but a little way on we would glimpse another which had pricked up its azure star in front of us in the grass. Some made so bold as to come and plant themselves by the side of the road, and a whole constellation began to take shape, what with my distant memories and these domesticated flowers. We began to go down the hill; and then we would meet, climbing it on foot, on a bicycle, in a cart or carriage, one of those creatures - flowers of a fine day but unlike the flowers of the field - a farm girl driving her cow or reclining on the back of a wagon, a shopkeeper's daughter taking the air, a fashionable young lady erect on the back seat of a landau, facing her parents. And even if I were fated now that I was ill and did not go out by myself, never to be able to make love to them, I was happy all the same, like a child born in a prison or hospital who, having long supposed that the human organism was capable of digesting only dry bread and medicines, has learned suddenly that peaches, apricots, and grapes are not simply part of the decoration of the country scene but delicious food. Even if his jailer or his nurse does not allow him to pluck those tempting fruits, still the world seems to him a better place. For a desire seems to us more attractive when we know that outside ourselves there is a reality which conforms to it even if, for us, it is not to be realized. As to the pretty girls who went past, from the day on which I had first know their cheeks could be kissed, I had become curious about their souls and the universe had appeared more interesting.

Mme de Villeparisis's carriage moved fast. I scarcely had time to see the girl who was coming in our direction; and yet I felt the desire not to let this girl pass without forcing her mind to become aware of my person, without preventing her desires from wandering to someone else, without insinuating myself into her dreams and taking possession of her heart. Meanwhile our carriage had moved on; the pretty girl was already behind us; and as she had-of me-none of those notions which constitute a person in one's mind, her eyes, which had barely seen me, had forgotten me already. Was it because I had caught but a momentary glimpse of her that I had found her so attractive? It may have been. In the first place, the impossibility of stopping when we meet a woman, the risk of not meeting her again another day, give her at once the same charm as a place derives from the illness or poverty that prevents us from visiting it, or the lustreless days which remain to us to live from the battle in which we shall doubtless fall. So that, if there were no such thing as habit, life must appear delightful to those of us who are continually under the threat of death-that is to say, to all mankind. Our imagination is set going by the desire for what we cannot possess. If night is falling and the carriage is moving fast, there is not a single torso that does not aim at our heart, from every crossing, from the lighted interior of every shop, the arrows of Beauty overstimulated by regret.

Had I been free to get down from the carriage and to speak to the girl whom we were passing, I might perhaps have been disillusioned. But they would never let me get out of the carriage, and I must add the pretty girl to the collection of all those whom I promised myself I would examine more closely at a later date. One of them however, happened to pass more than once before my eyes. This was a milk-girl who came from a farm with cream for the hotel. I fancied that she recognized me also.

Next day, a day on which I had been resting all

morning, when Francoise came in about noon to draw my curtains, she handed me a letter which had been left for me. I knew no one at Balbec. I had no doubt the letter was from the milk-girl. Alas it was only from Bergotte who, as he happened to be passing, had tried to see me, but on hearing that I was asleep had scribbled a few charming lines which I had supposed to have been written by the milk-girl. I was bitterly disappointed, and the thought it was more difficult and flattering to get a letter from Bergotte did not console me. As for the girl, I never came across her again, any more than I came across those I had seen from Mme de Villeparisis's carriage. Seeing and then losing them all thus increased the state of agitation in which I was living and I found a certain wisdom in the philosophers who recommend us to set a limit to our desires. At the same time I was inclined to regard this wisdom as incomplete, for I told myself that these encounters made me find even more beautiful a world which thus caused to grow along all the country roads flowers at once rare and common, and which gave a new zest to life.

On the day when Mme de Villeparisis took us to Carqueville to see the ivy-covered church of which she had spoken and which, built upon rising ground, dominated both the village and the river that flowed beneath it with its little medieval bridge, my grandmother, thinking that I would like to be left alone to study the building at my leisure, suggested to her friend that they should go on and wait for me at the pastry-cook's.

As I came away from the church I saw by the old bridge a cluster of girls from the village who, probably because it was Sunday, were standing about in their best clothes, hailing the boys who went past. One of them, a tall girl not so well dressed as the others but seeming to enjoy some ascendancy over them – for she scarcely answered when they spoke to her – with a more serious and a more self-willed air, was sitting on the parapet of the bridge with her feet hanging down, and holding on her lap a bowl full of fish she had presumably just caught. She had a tanned complexion, soft eyes but with a look of disdain for her surroundings, and a small nose, delicately and attractively modeled. My eyes alighted upon her skin, and my lips, at a pinch, might have believed they had followed my eyes. But it was not only her body I should have liked to attain; it was also the person that lived inside it, and with which there is but one form of contact, namely to attract its attention.

And this inner being of the handsome fisher-girl seemed to be still closed to me; I was doubtful whether I had entered it, even after I had seen my own image furtively reflected in the twin mirrors of her gaze, as if I had been placed in the field of vision of a doe. Meanwhile I could see, within a stone's throw, the square in which Mme de Villeparisis's carriage must be waiting for me.

We came down towards Hudimesnil; and suddenly I was overwhelmed with that profound happiness which I had not often felt since Combray, a happiness analogous to that which had been given me by the steeples of Martinville. But this time it remained incomplete. I had just seen, standing a little way back from the road along which we were travelling, three trees which formed a pattern I was not seeing for the first time. I could not succeed in reconstructing the place, but I felt it had been familiar to me once so that, my mind having wavered between some distant year and the present moment, Balbec and its surroundings began to dissolve and I wondered whether the whole of this drive were not make believe, Balbec a place to which I had never gone, Mme de Villeparisis a character in a story and the three old trees the reality which one recaptures on raising one's eyes from the book.

I looked at the three trees; I could see them plainly, but my mind felt they were concealing something, as when an object is out of reach so that our fingers, stretched out at arm's length, can only touch for a moment its outer surface without managing to take hold. Then we rest for a while before thrusting out with renewed momentum and trying to reach an inch further. But if my mind was thus to collect itself, to gather momentum, I should have to be alone. I recognized that kind of pleasure which requires a certain effort on the part of the mind. That pleasure, the object of which I could only dimly feel, which I must create for myself, I experienced only on rare occasions, but on each of these it seemed to me the things that had happened in the meantime were of little importance and in attaching myself to the reality of that pleasure alone could I at length begin to lead a true life.

I put my hand for a moment across my eyes, so as to be able to shut them without Mme de Villeparisis's noticing. I sat there thinking of nothing, then with my thoughts collected, compressed and strengthened, I sprang further forward in the direction of the trees, in that inner direction at the end of which I could see them inside myself. I felt again behind them the same object, known to me and yet vague, which I could not bring nearer. Where had I looked at them before? There was no place near Combray where an avenue opened off the road like that. Was I to suppose, then, they came from years already so remote in my life the landscape which

110

surrounded them had been obliterated from my memory and that, like the pages which, with a sudden thrill, we recognise in a book we imagined we had never read, they alone survived from the forgotten book of my earliest childhood? Or were they merely an image freshly extracted from a dream of the night before, but already so worn, so faded that it seemed to me to come from somewhere far more distant? Or had I indeed never seen them before, so that whereas they were inviting me to probe a new thought, I imagined I had to identify an old memory? Or again, were they concealing no hidden thought, and was it simply visual fatigue that made me see them double in time as one sometimes sees double in space? I could not tell. And meanwhile they were coming towards me; perhaps some fabulous apparition. I chose rather to believe they were phantoms of the past, companions of my childhood, vanished friends who were invoking our common memories. Like ghosts they seemed to be appealing to me to take them with me, to bring them back to life.

Presently, at a cross-roads, the carriage left them. It was bearing me away from what alone I believed to be true, what would have made me truly happy; it was like my life. I watched the trees gradually recede, waving their despairing arms, seeming to say to me: "What you fail to learn from us today you will never know. If you allow us to drop back into the hollow of this road from which we sought to raise ourselves up to you, a whole part of yourself which we were bringing to you will vanish for ever." And when, the road having forked and the carriage with it, I turned my back on them and ceased to see them, while Mme de Villeparisis asked me what I was dreaming about, I was as wretched as if I had just lost a friend.

It was time to be thinking of home. Mme de Villeparisis told her coachman to take us back by the old Balbec road.

15

Mme gave us warning that presently she would not be able to see so much of us. A young nephew who was preparing for Saumur and was meanwhile stationed in the neighbourhood at Doncieres was coming to spend a few weeks leave with her and she would be devoting most of her time to him. In the course of our drives together she had spoken highly of his intelligence and above all his kindheartedness and already I imagined that he would take a liking to me, that I should be his friend. One afternoon along the gangway leading from the beach to the road I saw approaching, tall, slim, bare necked, his head held proudly, a young man with penetrating eyes whose skin was as fair and his hair as golden as if they had absorbed all the rays of the sun. Dressed in a suit of soft, whitish material such as I could never have believed any man would wear, he was walking fast. His eyes were the color of the sea. Everyone looked at him as he passed, knowing this young Marquis de Saint-Loup-en-Bray was famed for his elegance. All the newspapers had described the suit in which he had recently acted as second to the young Duc d'Uzes in a duel. One felt that the distinctive quality of his hair, his eyes, his skin, his bearing must correspond to a life different from that led by other men. The prettiest women in society had disputed the possession of him. Because of his extraordinary good looks, some even thought him effeminate looking, though without holding it against him since they knew he was passionately fond of women. This was the nephew. He was coming from the beach, and the sea which filled the lower half of the glass front of the hall made a background against which he stood out. A carriage and pair awaited him at the door and, with the elegance and mastery which a great pianist contributes to display in the simplest stroke of execution, Mme de Villeparisis's nephew, while opening a letter, started up his horses.

How disappointed I was on the days that followed when, each time I met him outside or in the hotel I was forced to acknowledge that he had evidently no desire to make our acquaintance. Calling to mind the friendliness Mme de Villeparisis and M de Norpois had shown me, I thought perhaps they were only mock aristocrats and there must be a secret article that allowed women and certain diplomats to discard the haughtiness which must be pitilessly maintained by a young Marquis. My intelligence might have told me the opposite. But the characteristic feature of the ridiculous age I was going through is that we do not consult our intelligence and that the most trivial attributes of people seem to us to form an inseparable part of their personality. In a world thronged with monsters and gods, we know little peace of mind. There is hardly a single action we perform in that phase which we would not give anything, in later life, to be able to annul, whereas what we ought to regret is that we no longer possess the spontaneity which made us perform them. In later life we look at things in a more practical way, in full conformity with the rest of society, but adolescence is the only period in which we learn anything.

This insolence which I surmised in M. de Saint-Loup received confirmation whenever he passed us, his body as inflexibly erect as ever, his head held as high, his gaze as impassive, devoid of that vague respect one has for other people. When Mme de Villeparisis spoke to us of the inexhaustible kindness of her great-nephew (he was the son of one of her nieces, and a little older than myself), I marveled how the gentry, with an utter disregard of truth, ascribe tenderness of heart to people whose hearts are in reality hard and dry. Mme de Villeparisis herself confirmed, though indirectly, my diagnosis of her nephew's character one day when I met them both coming along a path so narrow she could not do otherwise than introduce me to him. He seemed not to hear; not a muscle of his face moved. Then, fastening on me those hard eyes as though he wished to examine me before returning my salute, keeping between himself and me the greatest possible interval, he stretched his arm out to its full extension and offered me his hand. I supposed that it must mean, at the very least, a duel when, next day, he sent me his card. But he spoke to me when we met only of literature, and declared after a long talk that he would like immensely to spend several hours with me every day. He had not only, in this encounter, given proof of an ardent zest for the things of the mind; he had shown a regard for me which was little in keeping with his greeting of the day before. The first rites or exorcism once performed, I saw this disdainful creature become the most friendly, most considerate young man I had ever met.

This young man who had the air of a disdainful aristocrat and sportsman had in fact no respect or curiousity except for the things of the mind, and especially those modern manifestations of literature and art which seemed ridiculous to his aunt; he was imbued, moreover, with what she called 'socialistic spoutings', was filled with the most profound contempt for his caste, and spent long hours in the study of Nietzsche and Proudhon.

From the first Saint-Loup made a conquest of my grandmother, not only by the incessant kindness which he went out of his way to show to us both, but by the naturalness he put into it as into everything else. For naturalness was the quality my grandmother preferred to all others, whether in gardens where she did not like too formal flower-beds, or in cooking where she detested dressed-up dishes, or in piano-playing which she did not like too polished, having indeed a special weakness for Rubinstein. She appreciated this rich young man still more highly for the free and careless way that he had of living in luxury without giving himself airs, she even discovered the incapacity Saint-Loup had of preventing his face from reflecting every emotion. Something not expected, if only a compliment, induced in him a pleasure so quick, so glowing, so volatile, so expansive that it was impossible for him to conceal it; a grin of delight seized irresistible hold of his face, and my grandmother was infinitely touched by this charming show of innocence. It was promptly settled between us that he and I were to be great friends for ever and he would say "our friend-ship" as though he were speaking of some important thing which he soon called - apart from his love for his mistress - the great joy of his life.

Saint-Loup could not leave the hotel, where he was expecting an uncle who was coming to spend a few days with Mme de Villeparisis. The uncle in question was called Palamède, a Christian name that had come down to him from his ancestors the Princes of Sicily. Saint-Loup told me that even in the most exclusive society his uncle Palamède stood out as being particularly unapproachable. At the Jockey Club he had, with a few of his friends, marked a list of two hundred members whom they would never allow to be introduced. And in the Comte de Paris's circle he was known by the nickname "the Prince" because of his elegance and his pride.

The morning after Robert had told me all these things about his uncle, while waiting for him as I was passing the Casino alone on my way back to the hotel, I had the sensation of being watched by somebody who was not far off. I turned my head and saw a man of about forty, very tall and rather stout, with a black moustache, who was staring at me. I took him at one moment for a thief and at another for a lunatic. And yet his scrupulously ordered attire was far more sober and far more simple than that of any of the summer visitors I saw at Balbec. My grandmother was coming towards me, we took a turn together, and I was waiting for her an hour later outside the hotel in which she had gone for a moment, when I saw emerge from it Mme de Villeparisis with Robert de Saint Loup and the stranger who had stared at me so intently.

"How are you? Let me introduce my nephew, the Baron de Guermantes" Mme de Villeparisis said to me, while the stranger, without looking at me, muttering a vague "Charmed!" and held out to me his middle and ring fingers, which I clasped through his suede glove; then, without lifting his eyes to my face, he turned towards Mme de Villeparisis. "Good gracious, I shall be forgetting my own name next!" she exclaimed with a laugh "Here am I calling you Baron de Guermantes. Let me introduce the Baron de Charlus. But after all, it's not a very serious mistake" she went on "for you're a thorough Guermantes all the same"

Leaving my grandmother, Mme de Villeparisis and him to talk to one another, I fell behind with Saint-Loup. "Tell me, am I right in thinking I heard Mme de Villeparisis say just now to your uncle that he was a Guermantes?"

"Of course he is: Palamède de Guermantes."

"Not the same Guermantes who have a place near Combray, and claim descent from Genevieve de Brabant?"

"Most certainly."

So she was related, and very closely, to the Guermantes, this Mme de Villeparisis who had for so long been for me the lady who had given me a duck filled with chocolates when I was small.

"Haven't they got the busts of all the old lords of Guermantes down there?"

"Yes, and a lovely sight they are!" Saint-Loup was ironical. "But what they have got which is a little more interesting, is quite a touching portrait of my aunt by Carriere. There are also some stunning pictures by Gustave Moreau. My aunt is the niece of your friend Mme de Villeparisis; she was brought up by her and married her cousin."

"Then what is your uncle?"

"He bears the title of Baron de Charlus. But you mustn't ask me to talk pedigrees. I know nothing more deadly, more outdated; really, life's too short."

I now recognised in the hard look which had made me turn round outside the Casino the same that I had seen fixed on me at Tansonville at the moment when Mme Swann had called Gilberte away.

"Wasn't Mme Swann one of the numerous mistresses you told me your uncle M de Charlus had?"

"Good lord, no! That is to say, my uncle's a great friend of Swann, and has always stood up for him. But no one has ever suggested that he was his wife's lover. You would cause the utmost astonishment in Parisian society if people thought you believed that."

I dared not reply that it would have caused even greater astonishment in Combray society if people had thought I did not believe it.

When, some days after, my grandmother told me with a joyful air that Saint-Loup had asked her whether she would like him to take a photograph of her before he left Balbec, and when I saw that she had put on her nicest dress for the purpose and was hesitating between various hats, I felt a little annoyed at this childishness, which surprised me on her part. I even wondered whether I did not put her on too lofty a pedestal, whether she was as unconcerned about her person as I had always supposed, whether she was entirely innocent of the weakness which I had always thought most alien to her, namely vanity. My grandmother, noticing I seemed put out, said that if her sitting for her photograph offended me in any way she would give up the idea. I would not hear of it. I assured her I saw no harm in it and let her adorn herself but, thinking to show how shrewd and forceful I was, added a few sarcastic and wounding words calculated to neutralise the pleasure she seemed to find in being photographed, with the result that I succeeded in driving from her face that joyful expression which ought to have made me happy. Alas, it too often happens, while the people we love best are still alive, that such expressions appear to us as the exasperating manifestation of some petty whim rather than as the precious form of the happiness which we should dearly like for them.

My ill humour arose more particularly from the fact that, during the week, my grandmother had appeared

to be avoiding me, and I had not been able to have her
to myself. When I came back in the afternoon I was
told that she was not in the hotel; or else she would
shut herself up with Francoise. And when, after being
out all evening with Saint-Loup, I had been thinking on
the way home of the moment at which I should be able
to embrace her, I waited in vain for her to give the three
little knocks on the wall which would tell me to go in
and say good night. At length I would go to bed, a little
resentful of her for depriving me, and I would lie there
for a while, my heart throbbing as in my childhood,
listening to the wall which remained silent, until I cried
myself to sleep.

16

Saint-Loup had been obliged to go to Doncieres where, until he returned there for good, he would be on duty now until late every afternoon. Left to myself, I was simply hanging about in front of the Grand Hotel until it was time for me to join my grandmother when, still almost at the far end of the esplanade, along which they projected a striking patch of colour, I saw five or six young girls as different in appearance and manner from all the people one was accustomed to see at Balbec as would have been a flock of gulls. One of these unknown girls was pushing a bicycle in front of her; two others carried golf-clubs; and their attire generally was in striking contrast to that of the other girls at Balbec some of whom, it was true, went in for sports but without adopting a special outfit.

It was the hour at which ladies and gentlemen came out every day for a stroll along the front. In the midst of all these people, the girls whom I had noticed, with the control of gesture that comes from the perfect suppleness of one's own body and a sincere contempt for the rest of humanity, were advancing straight ahead, without hesitation or stiffness, each of their limbs completely independent of the others, the rest of the body preserving that immobility which is so noticeable in good waltzers. They were now quite near me. Although each was different from the others, they all had beauty; but to tell the truth I had seen them for so short a time that I had not yet individualised any of them except for one, whose straight nose and dark complexion singled her out from the rest. And this want, in my vision, of the demarcations which I should presently establish between them permeated the group with a sort of shimmering harmony.

It was not perhaps mere chance in life that, in forming this group of friends, had chosen them all so beautiful; perhaps these girls (whose demeanor was enough to reveal their bold natures) had naturally felt a certain repulsion for all those companions in whom a pensive or sensitive disposition was betrayed by shyness, while attaching themselves to others, to whom they were drawn by grace and physical elegance.

For an instant as I passed the dark one with the plump cheeks who was wheeling a bicycle, I caught her smiling glance, aimed from the center of that inhuman world which enclosed the life of this little tribe, an unknown world wherein the idea of what I was could certainly never find a place. Wholly occupied with what her companions were saying, had she seen me - this young girl in the polo cap pulled down low over her forehead -

at the moment in which the dark ray emanating from her eyes had fallen on me? If she had seen me, what could I have represented to her?

If we thought the eyes of a girl were merely two glittering sequins, we should not be athirst to know her and unite her life to ours. But we sense that what shines in those discs is not their material; it is the ideas that person cherishes, the home to which she will return, the plans she is forming; and above all that it is she, with her desires, her sympathies, her revulsions, her will.

Was, then, the happiness of knowing these girls unattainable? Certainly the pleasure I derived from the little band had something of the fleetingness of passing figures on the road. This evanescence of persons who are not known to us urges us into that state of pursuit in which there is no longer anything to stem the tide of imagination. To strip our pleasures of imagination is to reduce them to their own dimensions, that is to say to nothing. We need imagination, awakened by uncertainty. We need, between us and the fish, the intervention, during our afternoons with the rod, of the rippling eddy, the bright gleam of flesh, the hint of a form in the fluidity of a transparent and mobile azure.

These girls benefited also by that alteration of social proportions characteristic of seaside life. Never, among actresses or peasants or convent girls, had I seen anything so beautiful, with so much that was unknown, so precious, so apparently inaccessible. I wondered whether the girls lived at Balbec, and who they could be. I had heard a lady say on the esplanade; "She's a friend of the Simonet girl" with that self-important air of inside knowledge.

I went indoors because I was to dine at Rivebelle with Robert, and my grandmother insisted that on those evenings, before going out, I must lie down for an hour on my bed. I asked the lift boy whether he knew of any people at Balbec called Simonet. Not liking to admit there was anything he did not know, he replied that he seemed to have heard the name somewhere. When we reached the top floor I asked him to send me the list of visitors.

I did not know which of these girls was Mlle Simonet, if indeed any of them was so named, but I did know that with Saint-Loup's help I was going to try to get to know her. But I had been wrong in hoping to excite curiosity in Saint-Loup by speaking to him of my band of girls. For it would remain paralysed in him by the actress whose lover he was. And even if he had felt it lightly stirring within him he would have repressed it, from an almost superstitious belief that on his own fidelity might depend that of his mistress. So it was without any promise from him that he would take an active interest in my girls that we set off to dine at Rivebelle.

On the first few occasions, when we arrived there, the sun would just have set, but it was light still; in the garden outside the restaurant, where the lamps had not yet been lighted, the heat of the day was falling and settling as though in a vase. Presently it was after nightfall when we alighted from the carriage, often indeed when we started from Balbec if the weather was bad and we had put off sending for the carriage in the hope of a lull. But on those days it was with no sense of gloom that I listened to the wind howling, for I knew that in the great dining room of the restaurant the innumerable lamps would triumph easily over the darkness and the cold, and I climbed light-heartedly after Saint-Loup into the closed carriage.

Our doctor having thought it prudent to warn me of the grave risks to which my state of health might expose me, I subordinated all my pleasures to an object which I judged to be infinitely more important, that of becoming strong enough to be able to bring into being the work which I had, possibly, within me, and had been exercising over myself, ever since I had come to Balbec, a scrupulous and constant control. Nothing would have induced me to touch the cup of coffee which would have robbed me of sleep. But when we arrived at Rivebelle, immediately - what with the excitement of a new pleasure, and finding myself in that different zone into which the exceptional introduces us after having cut the thread - patiently spun throughout so many days - that was guiding us towards wisdom; as though there were never to be any such thing as tomorrow, nor any lofty aims to be realised, all that prudent hygiene vanished. A waiter was offering to take my coat, whereupon Saint-Loup asked: "You're sure you won't be cold? It's not very warm in here."

"No, no," I assured him, and perhaps I did not feel the cold; but however that might be, I no longer knew the fear of falling ill, the necessity of not dying, the importance of work. I gave up my coat; we entered the dining room to the sound of some warlike march played by the band, we advanced between rows of tables as along an easy path of glory. From that moment I was a new man. The dose of beer and champagne, which at Balbec I should not take in a week, I now imbibed at a sitting, adding to it a few drops of port, and I gave the violinist the two louis I had been saving up for the last month.

The alcohol I had drunk had given the moment a charm, making me prefer it a thousand times to the rest of my life. I was enclosed in the present, my past no longer projected before me that shadow of itself we call our future. I knew none of the women who were at Rivebelle and who, because they were part of my intoxication, appeared to me a thousand times more desirable. One of them, young, fair, alone, with a sad expression, gazed at me for a moment. Then it was the turn of another, and a third, finally of a dark one with glowing cheeks. Almost all of them were known to Saint-Loup. On the way back to Balbec, of this or that charmer to whom he had introduced me I would repeat to myself almost unconsciously: "What a delightful woman!" as one sings a refrain. True, these words were prompted rather by overexcitement than by lasting judgment. When the hours of our lives unfold on disparate planes, we give away too much of ourselves to all sorts of people who next day will not interest us in the least.

Presently Saint-Loup's visit drew to an end. I had not seen those girls again on the beach. He was too little at Balbec in the afternoons to have time to attempt, in my interest, to make their acquaintance. In the evenings he was freer, and continued to take me regularly to Rivebelle. Two or three times already in the restaurant, Saint-Loup and I had seen a man of large stature, muscular, with a grizzled beard, come in and sit down, his pensive gaze fixed upon the void. One evening, on our asking the landlord who this solitary diner was, he exclaimed "What! Do you mean to say you don't know the famous painter Elstir?" Swann had once mentioned his name to me, I had forgotten in what connexion; but the omission of a particular memory leads sometimes not to uncertainty but to the birth of a premature certainty. "He's a friend of Swann's and a very well known artist, extremely good" I told Saint-Loup. Immediately the thought swept through us like a thrill, that Elstir was a great artist, a celebrated man, and that he had no suspicion of the excitement into which we were plunged by the idea of his talent. Since we were still at an age when enthusiasm cannot keep silence, and anonymity is suffocating, we wrote a letter, signed with both our names, in which we revealed to Elstir two passionate admirers of his talent, two friends of his great friend Swann, and asked to be allowed to pay homage to him in person. A waiter undertook to convey this missive to the celebrity.

We watched him read our letter, put it in his pocket, finish his dinner, get up to go; and we were so convinced we had offended him by our overture we would now have hoped (as keenly as at first we had dreaded) to make our escape without his noticing us. What did not cross our minds was that our enthusiasm for Elstir was not, as we imagined it to be, admiration, since neither of us had ever seen anything he had painted. It was, at most, admiration in the abstract, the sentimental framework of an admiration without content, that is to say a thing attached to boyhood; we were still boys. Elstir meanwhile was approaching the door when suddenly he turned and came towards us. I was overcome by a delicious thrill of terror such as I could not have felt a few years later, because as age diminishes the capacity, familiarity with the world meanwhile destroys in us any inclination to provoke strange encounters, to feel that kind of emotion.

In the course of the few words Elstir came to say to us, sitting down at our table, he asked me to come and see him at his studio, an invitation which he did not extend to Saint-Loup, and which I had earned by a few words which made him think I was devoted to the arts. Compared with that of a great artist, the friendliness of a great nobleman, however charming it may be, seems like play acting. Saint-Loup sought to please; Elstir loved to give, to give himself. Everything he possessed; ideas, works, and the rest, he would have given gladly to anyone who understood him. But for lack of congenial company, he lived in an unsociable isolation which fashionable people called ill-breeding, his neighbours madness, his family selfishness.

17

My grandmother, whom I told of my meeting with Elstir and who rejoiced at the intellectual profit I might derive from his friendship; considered it absurd and none too polite of me not to pay him a visit. But I could think only of the little band, and being uncertain of the hour at which the girls would be passing along the front, I dared not absent myself. I seized every pretext for going down to the beach at the hours when I hoped to succeed in finding them. I loved none of them, loving them all, and yet the possibility of meeting them was in my life the sole element of delight, aroused in me hopes ending often in fury if I had not seen them. Meanwhile my grandmother, because I now showed a keen interest in golf and tennis and was letting slip an opportunity of seeing an artist whom she knew to be one of the greatest of his time, evinced for me a scorn which seemed based on somewhat narrow views. I had guessed long ago, in the Champs-Elysees, that the emotions which a perfectly ordinary girl arouses in us can bring to the surface parts of our being more personal than any we derive from the conversation of a great man or even from the admiration of his work.

I finally had to comply with my grandmother's wishes, all the more reluctantly in that Elstir lived at some distance from the front in one of the newest avenues. I endeavored not to look at the gimcrack splendour of the buildings, among which Elstir's villa was perhaps the most sumptuously hideous, in spite of which he had taken it because, of all there were to be had at Balbec, it was the only one with a really big studio.

At the moment I entered the creator was just finishing the outline of the setting sun. The blinds were closed almost everywhere round the studio, which was fairly cool and, except in one place where daylight laid against the wall its brilliant decoration, dark. One small rectangular window was open, embowered in honeysuckle and giving on to an avenue beyond a strip of garden; so the atmosphere of the greater part of the studio was dusky, but liquid and sparkling at the edges where the sunlight encased it, like a lump of rock crystal of which one surface, cut and polished, gleams like a mirror. While Elstir, at my request, went on painting, I wandered about in the half-light, stopping to examine first one picture then another.

Naturally enough, what he had in his studio were almost all seascapes done here at Balbec. I was able to discern from these that the charm of each of them lay in a sort of metamorphosis of the objects represented, analogous to what in poetry we call metaphor, and that, if God the Father had created things by naming them, it was by taking away their names or giving them other names that Elstir created them anew.

Sometimes, at my window in the hotel, I had been led by some effect of the sunlight to mistake what was only a darker stretch of the sea for a distant coastline, or to gaze delightedly at a belt of liquid azure without knowing whether it belonged to sea or sky. But presently reason would reestablish. In the same way from my bedroom in Paris I would sometimes hear a dispute in the street below, until I had traced back to its cause - a carriage for instance that was rattling towards me - that noise from which I now eliminated the vociferations my ear had really heard but which my reason knew the wheels did not produce. But the moments in which we see nature poetically were those from which Elstir's work was created. It was, for instance, for a metaphor of this sort - in a picture of the harbor of Carquethuit, that houses concealed a part of the harbor, the roofs overtopped by masts, making the vessels appear built on land. On the beach in the foreground men pushing their boats were running as much through the waves as along the sand which, being wet, reflected the hulls as if they were in the water. The sea itself did not come up in an even line but followed the irregularities of the shore, which the perspective of the picture increased still further, so that a ship actually at sea seemed to be sailing through the middle of the town.

It is said there can be no progress in art, only in the sciences, and each artist starting afresh cannot be either helped or hindered by the efforts of any other. The effort made by Elstir to reproduce things not as he knew them to be but according to the optical illusions of our first sight had led him to bring out certain laws of perspective, which were all the more striking since art had been the first to disclose them. A river, because of the windings of its course, a bay because of the apparent proximity to the cliffs on either side of it, would seem to have hollowed out in the heart of the plain or the mountains a lake, landlocked on every side as, at the foot of immense cliffs, the grace of white sails on the blue mirror looked like sleeping butterflies. The effort made by Elstir to strip himself of every intellectual notion was all the more admirable in that this man who made himself deliberately ignorant before sitting down to paint had in fact an exceptionally cultivated mind.

The intellectual pleasures I was enjoying in this studio did not in the least prevent me from being aware, although they enveloped us, of the sparkling penumbra of the room itself and, through the little window framed with honeysuckle, the sun-parched earth and the shade of the trees. Perhaps the unconscious well-being induced by this summer day had surged in me at the sight of Elstir's *Carquethuit Harbour*.

Elstir and I had meanwhile been walking towards the end of the studio, and reached the window that looked across the garden on to a narrow side street. I looked out vaguely over this rustic path which passed quite close to the studio. Suddenly there appeared on it, coming toward us at a rapid pace, the young cyclist of the little band with her polo cap pulled down, her eyes gay and challenging; and I saw her, beneath the trees, address to Elstir the smiling greeting of a friend. She even came up to shake hands with the painter, and I saw she had a tiny beauty spot on her chin. "Do you know that girl, Monsieur?" I asked Elstir, realising that he might introduce me, and this peaceful studio with its rural horizon was at once filled with delight. Elstir told me she was called Albertine Simonet, and gave me the names also of her friends, whom I described to him.

"Not a day passes but one or other of them comes by here, and looks in for a minute or two" Elstir told me, plunging me into despair at the thought that if I had gone to see him at once, when my grandmother had begged me to, I should have made Albertine's acquaintance long since.

She continued on her way; I supposed that she had gone to join her friends on the front. If I could have been there with Elstir I should have got to know them. I thought up endless pretexts to induce him to take a stroll with me on the beach. He agreed to walk a few steps with me but said he must first finish the piece on which he was engaged. Elstir as he worked talked to me but I scarcely listened; he was now only the intermediary between these girls and me.

It was finished at last. And, once we were out of doors, I discovered that - so long were the days still at this season - it was not so late as I had supposed. We strolled down to the front. What strategems I employed to keep Elstir standing at the spot where I thought the girls might still come past!

Dusk was falling; it was time to turn homewards. I was accompanying Elstir back to his villa when suddenly, as Mephistopheles springing up before Faust, there appeared at the end of the avenue - like a simple objectification - the band of girls, who looked as though they had not seen me. Feeling that a meeting between them and us was now inevitable, and that Elstir would be certain to call me, I turned my back like a bather preparing to meet the shock of a wave; I stopped and, leaving my companion to pursue his way, remained where I was, stooping towards the window of the antique shop. I was already dimly aware that when Elstir did call me up to introduce me I should wear that sort of expression which betrays not surprise but the wish to look surprised - such bad actors are we, or such good mind-readers our fellow men - that I should even go so far as to point a finger to my breast, ask "are you calling me?" and join him, my face masking annoyance at being torn from the study of old pottery.

The certainty of being introduced to these girls had the effect of making me not only feign indifference to them, but actually feel it. Henceforth inevitable, the pleasure of knowing them began to contract. Elstir was about to call me. This was not at all the way in which I had so often imagined myself making the acquaintance of these girls. What was about to happen was different, I was not prepared. I regretted almost that I had come. The shrinking of the pleasure I had expected to feel was due to the certainty that nothing now could take it from me. And it recovered when it ceased to be subjected to certainty, at the moment when, having decided to turn my head, I saw Elstir bidding them good-bye. The face of the girl nearest him, round and glittering with the light in her eyes, reminded me of a cake on the top of which a place has been kept for a morsel of blue sky. For a moment her eyes met mine, like those traveling skies on stormy days. At the moment her gaze was coincident with mine it clouded over slightly, so on a clear night the wind swept moon passes behind a cloud for a moment.

Elstir left the girls without having summoned me. They disappeared down a side street; he came towards me. It was a fiasco.

That day at Balbec I learned for the first time that variations in the importance which a pleasure or sorrow has in our eyes may depend on invisible beliefs. It is true that something in me was aware of this role beliefs play; namely, my will; but its knowledge is vain if one's intelligence and one's sensibility continue in ignorance.

It was a piece of luck, all the same, they should have seen me in Elstir's company, and so could not forget me; also that I should have put on that morning, at my grandmother's suggestion, my smart waistcoat, when I might have been wearing one that was hideous. For while an event for which we are longing never happens quite in the way we have been expecting, we have been so dreading the worst that in the end we are inclined to feel that chance has, on the whole, been rather kind. The probability of now being able to meet the little band whenever I chose was all the more precious to me because I should not have been able to watch for them during the next few days, which were taken up with preparations for Saint-Loup's departure.

When, some days after, I had succeeded in persuading Elstir to give a small party at which I should meet Albertine, the freshness of appearance and elegance of attire which were to be observed in me at the moment of my starting out from the hotel were such that I regretted my inability to reserve them for the captivation of some other more interesting person. My brain assessed this pleasure at a low value, now that it was assured. While, at the moment we are about to start on an eagerly awaited journey, our intelligence and sensibility begin to ask themselves whether it is really worth the trouble, the will, knowing those lazy masters would at once begin to consider that journey wonderful if it became impossible for us to undertake it, leaves them arguing outside the station, vying with each other, but busies itself with buying the tickets and putting us into the carriage. My will would not let the hour pass, and it was Elstir's address that it called out to the driver.

This is not to say the introduction which followed did not give me any pleasure, but I was naturally not conscious of it until later when, back at the hotel, I had become myself again. Pleasure in this respect is like photography. What we take, in the presence of the beloved object, we develop later, when we have once again found that inner darkroom which is barred to us so long as we are with other people. At the moment when our name rings out on the lips of the introducer, she to whose presence we have been longing to attain vanishes; each constituent of imagination and desire giving place to a notion worth infinitely less, a notion to which, it is true, there was added presently a sort of equivalent, in the domain of real life.

And yet, whatever the inevitable disappointments it must bring, this movement towards what we have only glimpsed, what we have been free to dwell upon and imagine at our leisure, this movement is the only one that is wholesome for the senses. How drearily monotonous must be the lives of people who, from indolence or timidity, drive straight to the doors of friends without having first dreamed of knowing them, without ever daring, on the way, to stop and examine their desire!

18

Whatever my disappointment in finding in Mlle Simonet a girl so little different from those I knew already, I comforted myself with the thought that through Albertine at any rate, even if she herself was not all I had hoped, I might make the acquaintance of her comrades of the little band.

Shortly after this, one morning when it had been raining and was almost cold, I was accosted on the front by a girl wearing a toque and carrying a muff, so different from the girl whom I had met at Elstir's party that to recognise in her the same person seemed beyond the power of the mind. Mine was, however, successful in performing it, but after a moment's surprise which did not, I think, escape Albertine. On the other hand, I now experienced astonishment at her rude tone and manners.

"What weather!" she began "Really the perpetual summer of Balbec is all stuff and nonsense. Don't you do anything here? We never see you playing golf or dancing at the casino. You don't ride either. You must be bored stiff. You don't find it deadly, idling about on the beach all day? I can see you're not like me; I simply adore all sports. You weren't at the Sogne races? We went in the tram, and I can quite understand that you wouldn't see any fun in that. It took us two whole hours! I could have gone there and back three times on my bike."

I who had admired Saint-Loup when, in the most natural manner in the world, he had called the little local train the "crawler" because of the ceaseless windings of its line, was daunted by the glibness with which Albertine spoke of it as the "tram" and the "rattletrap." In speaking, Albertine kept her head motionless and her nostrils pinched, and scarcely moved her lips. The result was a juvenile affectation which, as it happened, soon disappeared when she knew people better, giving place to a naturally girlish tone. But to me it was peculiarly delightful. Whenever I had gone several days without seeing her, I would refresh my spirit by repeating to myself: "We don't ever see you playing golf," with the nasal intonation. And I thought then there was no one in the world so desirable.

We formed, that morning, one of those couples who dotted the front here and there. We met almost immediately the tall one, Andrée, and Albertine was obliged to introduce me. Her friend had extraordinarily bright eyes, like a glimpse through an open door of a room into which the sun is shining from the glittering sea. This Andrée, who had struck me when I first saw her as the coldest of them all, was infinitely more refined, more affectionate, more sensitive than Albertine, to whom she displayed the gentle tenderness of an elder sister. At the Casino she would come across the floor to sit down beside me and forgo a waltz or even, if I was tired, to give up the casino and come to me instead at the hotel.

There were days when we picnicked at one of the outlying farms which catered for visitors. These were the farms known as Les Ecorres, Marie-Therese, La Croix d'Heuland, Bagatell, Californie and Marie-Antoinette. It was the last that had been adopted by the little band. But at other times, instead of going to a farm, we would climb to the highest point of the cliff and undo our parcel of sandwiches and cakes. We ate our food, and if I had brought with me also some little keepsake which might appeal to one or other of my friends, joy sprang with such violence into their faces, flushed in an instant, that their lips, to allow it to escape, parted in a burst of laughter. They were gathered round me, and between their faces the air that separated them traced pathways such as might have been cut by a gardener wishing to create a little space to move through a thicket of roses. When we had finished eating we would play games which until then I should have thought boring, sometimes such childish games as King of the Castle, or Who Laughs First; not for a kingdom would I have renounced them now; the aurora of adolescence with which the faces of these girls still glowed, and from which I, young as I was, had already emerged, shed its light on everything around them. One saw only a charming glow of colour beneath which what in a few years time would be a profile was not discernible. It comes so soon, the moment when there is nothing left to wait for, when the body holds no fresh surprise. It is so short, that radiant morning time, continuously moulded by the fleeting impression of the moment. This plasticity gives a variety and charm to the attentions which a young girl pays us. Of course, such attentions are indispensable in the mature woman also, but these endearments, after a certain age, cease to send gentle ripples over faces which the struggle for existence has hardened. One-owing to the prolonged strain of the obedience that subjects wife to husband - will seem not so much a woman's face as a soldier's; another, carved by the sacrifices which a mother has to make, will be the face of an apostle. A third is, after a stormy passage through the years, the face of a mariner, upon a body of which its garments alone indicate the sex. Certainly the attentions a woman pays us can still, so long as we are in love with her, endue with fresh charms the hours we spend in her company. But she is not then for us a series of different women. Whereas adolescence precedes this solidification, and hence we feel, in the company of girls, the spectacle of forms undergoing change, a play of unstable forces which recalls the elements of nature we contemplate when we stand before the sea.

The same was true of Albertine as of her friends. On certain days, thin with a grey complexion, a sullen air, a violet transparency slanting across her eyes such as we notice sometimes on the sea, she seemed to be feeling the sorrows of exile. On other days her face, smoother and glossier, drew one's desires to its surface and prevented them going further. At other times, happiness bathed those cheeks with a radiance so mobile that the skin, grown fluid and vague, gave passage to a glaze which made it appear to be of another colour but not of another substance than the eyes. And each of these Albertines was different, as is each appearance of the dancer according to the varied play of a spotlight. It was perhaps because they were so diverse, that I developed the habit of becoming myself a different person, according to the particular Albertine to whom my thoughts had turned; jealous, indifferent, melancholy, frenzied, created not merely by accident but also of the belief in which I appreciated it. For this was the point to which I invariably had to return, to those beliefs which for most of the time occupy our souls unbeknown to us, but which are of more importance than the person whom we see, for it is through them that we see him.

I ought to give a different name to each of the selves who thought about Albertine; I ought still more to give a different name to each of the Albertines who appeared before me, never the same, like those seas - called by me simply "the sea" - against which she was silhouetted. But above all I ought always to give name to the belief that reigned over my soul on any given day I saw Albertine - the appearance of people, like that of the sea, being dependent on those clouds, barely visible, which change the colour of everything - like that cloud which Elstir had rent by not introducing me to these girls, whose images had suddenly appeared to me more beautiful when they moved away - a cloud that formed again a few days later when I did get to know them. I would gaze at those lovely forms, dark and fair, scattered around me on the grass as if, like young Hercules or Telemachus, I had been playing amid a band of nymphs.

19

Then the concerts ended, the bad weather began, my friends left Balbec. Not all at once like the swallows, but all in the same week. We had to leave at last, the cold and damp too penetrating for a hotel which had neither fireplaces nor central heating. I forgot almost immediately these last weeks of our stay. What I saw in my mind's eye when I thought of Balbec were the hours which, every morning during the fine weather, my grandmother insisted on my lying down with the room darkened. I knew that my friends were on the front but did not see them as they passed. I guessed their presence, heard their laughter in the soft surge of sound that rose to my ears. Twelve o'clock struck, and Francoise arrived at last. And for months on end, in this Balbec which I imagined only as battered by storms and buried in the mist, the weather had been so dazzling and so unchanging that when she came to open the window I could always, without once being wrong, expect to see the same patch of sunlight in the corner of the wall.

20 - THE GUERMANTES WAY

The twittering of the birds at daybreak sounded insipid
to Francoise. Every word uttered by the maids made
her jump; disturbed by all their running about, she kept
asking herself what they could be doing. In other
words, we had moved. True, the servants had made no
less commotion in the attics of our old home; but she
knew them, she had made of their comings and goings
something friendly and familiar. Now she listened to
the very silence with painful attentiveness. And as our
new neighbourhood appeared to be as quiet as the
boulevard on to which we had hitherto looked had been
noisy, the song of a passer-by brought tears to the eyes
of the exiled Francoise. Hence, if I had been tempted
to scoff at her when she had packed her trunks
weeping, on the other hand, finding it hard to assimilate
the new as I found it easy to abandon the old, I felt

myself drawn towards our old servant. She alone could understand what I was feeling. And so I went to Francoise who, in return for my having laughed at her tears over a departure which had left me cold, now showed an icy indifference to my sorrow. Francoise, who would not allow the least of her own ailments to pass unnoticed, if I were in pain would turn her head away so I should not have the satisfaction of seeing my suffering so much as observed. It was the same as soon as I tried to speak to her about our new house. Francoise came back saying she really thought she would stifle on our old boulevard, that she would not go back to live there for a king's ransom, and that everything was much better fitted up in our new home. Which, it is high time now the reader should be told - was a flat forming part of the Hotel de Guermantes.

As the word church signifies not only the temple but also the assembly of the faithful, this Hotel de Guermantes comprised all those who shared the life of the Duchess, but these intimates on whom I had never set eyes were for me only famous and poetic names and served to enhance and protect the mystery of the Duchess by extending all round her a vast halo which at most declined in brilliance as its circumference increased.

This vortex of names round that statuette which was Mme de Guermantes gave her mansion of glass the transparency of a showcase. After Saint-Loup had told me various anecdotes about his cousin's chaplain, her gardeners and the rest, the Hotel de Guermantes had become - as the Louvre might have been in days gone by - a kind of palace surrounded, in the very heart of Paris, by its own domains, acquired by virtue of an ancient right that had quaintly survived, over which she still enjoyed feudal privileges.

One day an old friend of my father said to us, speaking of the Duchess: "She has the highest position in the Faubourg Saint-Germain; hers is the leading house" and it became all the more essential that I should be able to explore the "salon" of Mme de Guermantes, among her friends. The life which I supposed them to lead there flowed from a source so different from anything in my experience and must, I felt, be so out of the ordinary that I could not have imagined the presence at the Duchess's parties of people in whose company I myself had already been, of people who really existed.

My father had a friend at the Ministry, One A.J. Moreau, who found himself in possession of a stall for a gala night at the Opera. He sent the ticket to my father and since Berma was to give an act of Phedre, my grandmother persuaded my father to pass it on to me.

That evening I took my seat, trying to recapture a line from Phedre which I could not quite remember. A certain number of orchestra stalls had been offered for sale at the box office and bought, out of snobbishness or curiosity, by such as wished to study the appearance of people whom they might not have another opportunity of seeing at close quarters. And it was indeed a fragment of their true social life, ordinarily concealed, that one could examine here in public. For the Princesse de Parme having herself distributed among her friends the seats in stall, balconies and boxes, the house was like a drawing-room in which everyone changed places, went to sit here or there, next to friends. In the boxes the white deities who inhabited those somber abodes had taken refuge against their shadowy walls and remained invisible. Gradually, however, as the performance went on, their vaguely human forms detached themselves languidly one after the other from the depths of the night and allowed their half-naked bodies to emerge into the chiaroscuro of the surface where their gleaming faces appeared behind the playful, frothy undulations of ostrich-feather fans; then, the act ended, having no further hope of hearing the melodious sounds of earth which had drawn them to the surface, plunging back all at once, vanished into the night.

Of all these retreated to the thresholds of which their frivolous desire to behold the works of man brought the curious goddesses who let none approach them, the most famous was the cube of semi-darkness known to the world as the stage box of the Princesse de Guermantes. Like a tall goddess presiding from afar over the frolics of lesser deities, the Princess had deliberately remained somewhat in the background on a sofa placed sideways in the box, red as a coral reef, beside a large vitreous expanse which was probably a mirror and suggested a section, perpendicular, opaque and liquid, cut by a ray of sunlight in the dazzling crystal of the sea. A great white flower, downy as the wing of a bird, hung from the Princess's forehead along one of her cheeks, the curve of which it followed with coquettish suppleness, as if half enclosing a pink egg in the softness of a halcyon's nest. Over her hair, reaching in front to her eyebrows and caught back lower down at the level of her throat, was spread a net composed of little white shells intermingled with pearls, a marine mosaic barely emerging from the depths of which a human presence was revealed by the glittering of the Princess's eyes. The beauty which set her far above all the other fabulous daughters of the twilight was not altogether inscribed in the nape of her neck, in her shoulders, her arms, her waist. But the exquisite, unfinished line of the last was the focus of invisible lines which the eye could not help prolonging - lines engendered round the woman like the spectre of an ideal figure projected against the darkness.

"That's the Princesse de Guermantes" said my neighbour to the gentleman beside her, "She hasn't been sparing with her pearls. I'm sure if I had as many as that I wouldn't make such a display of them; it doesn't look at all genteel to my mind." And yet, when they caught sight of the Princess, all those who were looking round to see who was in the audience felt the rightful throne of beauty rise up in their hearts. Like certain artists who, instead of the letters of their names, set at the foot of their canvases a figure that is beautiful in itself, a butterfly, a flower, so it was the figure of a face and body that the Princess affixed at the corner of her box.

Just as the curtain was rising I looked up at Mme de Guermantes's box. The Princess had just turned her head towards the back of her box; the guests were all on their feet and also turned towards the door, and between the double hedge which they thus formed, with all the triumphant assurance of the goddess that she was, the Duchesse de Guermantes entered. Instead of the wonderful downy plumage which descended from the crown of the Princess's head, instead of her net of shells and pearls, the Duchess wore in her hair only a simple aigrette. Her neck and shoulders emerged from a drift of snow white chiffon, against which fluttered a swansdown fan, but below this her gown moulded her figure with a precision that was positively British. Different as their two costumes were, after the Princess had given her cousin the chair in which she herself had previously been sitting, they could be seen turning to gaze at one another in mutual appreciation.

The Duchess had seen me once with her husband, but could surely have kept no memory of that, and I was not distressed that she should find herself gazing down upon the nameless collective audience, for I was happily aware that my being was dissolved in their midst when the Duchess, goddess turned woman, raised towards me the white-gloved hand which had been resting on the balustrade and waved it in token of friendship; my gaze was caught in the spontaneous incandescence of the flashing eyes of the Princess, who had unwittingly set them ablaze merely by turning her head to see who her cousin was greeting; and the latter, who had recognised me, poured upon me the sparkling shower of her smile.

21

Now, every morning, long before the hour at which she
left her house, I went by a devious route to post myself
at the corner of the street along which she generally
came and, when the moment of her arrival seemed
imminent, I strolled back with an air of being absorbed
in something else, and raised my eyes as I drew level
with her, as though I had not in the least expected to
see her. I was genuinely in love with Mme de
Guermantes. The greatest happiness that I could have
asked of God would have been that he should send
down on her every imaginable calamity and that,
ruined, despised, stripped of all privilege, having no
longer any home of her own or people who would
speak to her, she should come to me for asylum. I
imagined her doing so. I had, alas, in reality, chosen to
love the woman who in her own person combined
perhaps the greatest possible number of advantages; in
whose eyes, accordingly, I could not hope to cut any

sort of figure, for she was rich - and noble also; not to mention that personal charm which made her among the rest a sort of queen.

I felt that I displeased her by crossing her path every morning; but even if I had the heart to refrain from doing so for two or three days consecutively, Mme de Guermantes might not have noticed. And indeed I could not have brought myself to cease. To be for a moment the object of her attention, the person to whom her greeting was addressed, was stronger than my fear of arousing her displeasure.

I should never have had the heart to leave Paris except in a direction that would bring me closer to Mme de Guermantes. This was by no means an impossibility. Would I not indeed find myself nearer to her than I was in the morning, in the street, humiliated, in that weary time of my daily walks, which might go on indefinitely without getting me any further, if I were to go miles away but to someone of her acquaintance, someone whom she knew to be particular in the choice of his friends and who appreciated me, who might speak to her about me, and make her aware of what I wanted? The friendship and admiration that Saint-Loup had shown me seemed to me undeserved and had hitherto left me unmoved. All at once I set great store by them; I would have liked him to disclose them to Mme de Guermantes, was quite prepared even to ask him to do so. For when we are in love, we long to be able to divulge to the woman we love all the little privileges we enjoy, as the deprived and the tiresome do in everyday life.

Saint-Loup had not for a long time been able to come to Paris either, as he himself claimed, because of his military duties, or, as was more likely, because of the trouble he was having with his mistress, with whom he had twice now been on the point of breaking off. He had often told me what a pleasure it would be to him if I came to visit him in that garrison town the name of which, a couple of days after his leaving Balbec, had caused me so much joy when I read it on the envelope of the first letter I received from my friend. Not so far from Balbec as its inland surroundings might have led one to think, it was one of those little fortified towns set in a broad expanse of country over which on fine days there floats so often in the distance a sort of intermittent blur of sound which indicates the movements of a regiment on manoeuvre that the very atmosphere of its streets, avenues and squares has been gradually tuned to a sort of perpetual vibrancy. It was not too far away from Paris for me to be able, if I took the express, to return to my mother and grandmother and sleep in my own bed. As soon as I realised this, troubled by a painful longing, I had too little will-power to decide to stay in town; but also too little to prevent a porter from carrying my luggage to a cab and not to adopt, as I walked behind him, the complete detachment of a person who has the air of knowing what he wants, and not to give the driver the address of the cavalry barracks. I thought that Saint-Loup might come and sleep that night in the hotel, in order to make the first shock of this strange town less painful for me.

One of the guard went to find him, and I waited at the barracks gate, in front of that huge ship of stone, booming with the November wind, out of which, for it was now six o'clock, men were emerging in pairs into the street as if they were coming ashore in some exotic port.

Saint-Loup appeared, moving like a whirlwind. I had not given my name and was eager to enjoy his surprise and delight. "Oh what a bore!" he exclaimed, suddenly catching sight of me, "I've just had a week's leave and I shan't be off duty again for another week." And he knitted his brows with vexation. "Run along and light the fire in my quarters" he called to a trooper who passed by "Hurry up, get a move on."

Then once more he turned towards me and once more his peering gaze testified to our great friendship. "No really, you here, in these barracks, I can scarcely believe my eyes, I feel I must be dreaming! But how is your health? A little better, I hope. You must tell me all about yourself presently. We'll go up to my room; we mustn't hang about too long on the square, there's the devil of a wind. I don't feel it now myself, but you aren't accustomed to it, I'm afraid of your catching cold. And what about your work? Have you settled down to it yet? No? You are an odd fellow! If I had your talent I'm sure I should be writing morning, noon and night. It amuses you more to do nothing. What a pity it is that it's the second-raters like me who are always ready to work, while the ones who could don't want to! There and I've clean forgotten to ask how your grandmother is. Her Proudhon never leaves me."

A tall, handsome, majestic officer emerged with slow and solemn steps from the foot of a staircase. "I must say a word to the Captain, be a good fellow and go and wait for me in my room. It's the second on the right, on the third floor. I'll be with you in a minute." I started to climb the staircase, catching glimpses of barrack-rooms, their bare walls bordered with a double line of beds and kits. I was shown Saint-Loup's room. I stood for a moment outside its closed door, for I could hear movement - something stirring, something being dropped. I felt the room was not empty, that there was somebody there. But it was only the freshly lighted fire beginning to burn. It could not keep quiet; shifting its logs about clumsily. As I entered the room, it let one roll into the fender and set another smoking. And even when it was not moving, like an ill bred person it made noises all the time which, from the moment I saw the flames rising, revealed themselves to me as noises made by a fire, although if I had been on the other side of a wall I should have thought they came from someone blowing his nose and walking about. I sat down and waited.

The door opened and Saint-Loup rushed in, dropping his monocle.

"Ah, Robert, how comfortable it is here, how good it would be if one were allowed to dine and sleep here."

And indeed, had it not been against the regulations, what repose untinged by sadness I could have enjoyed there, guarded by that atmosphere of tranquility, vigilance and gaiety which was maintained by a thousand ordered and troubled wills, a thousand carefree minds, in that great community called a barracks.

"So you'd rather stay with me, would you, than go to the hotel by yourself?" Saint-Loup asked me, smiling. "Well you flatter me!" he replied "because it actually occurred to me that you'd rather stay here tonight and that is precisely what I went to ask the Captain."

"And he has given you leave?"

"He hadn't the slightest objection. Now, let me just get hold of my batman and tell him to see about our dinner"

We were several times interrupted by the entry of one or other of Saint-Loup's comrades. He drove them all out again, I begged him to let them stay.

"No really, they would bore you stiff. They're absolutely uncouth people who can talk of nothing but racing or stable shop. Mind you, when I tell you these fellows are brainless, it isn't that everything military is devoid of intellectuality. Far from it. We have a major here who's an admirable man. He's given us a course in which military history is treated like a demonstration, like a problem in algebra. Even from the aesthetic point of view there's a curious beauty, alternately inductive and deductive about it, which you couldn't fail to appreciate."

Soon I was going to see the regiment doing field manoeuvres. I began to take an interest in the military theories which Saint-Loup's friends used to expound over the dinner table, and it had become the chief desire of my life to see at close quarters their various leaders, just as a person who makes music his principal study and spends his life in the concert halls finds pleasure in frequenting the cafes in which one can share the life of the members of the orchestra. To reach the training ground I used to have to make long journeys on foot. In the evening after dinner the longing for sleep made my head droop every now and then as in a fit of vertigo. Next morning I realized I had not heard the band any more than, at Balbec, after the evenings on which Saint Loup had taken me to dinner at Rivebelle, I used to hear the concert on the beach. And when I wanted to get up I had a delicious sensation of being incapable of doing so; I felt myself fastened to a deep, invisible soil by the articulations (of which my tiredness made me conscious) of muscular and nutritious roots. I felt myself full of strength; life seemed to extend more simply before me; for I had reverted to the healthy tiredness of my childhood at Combray on mornings after the days when we had taken the Guermantes walk.

Poets claim that we recapture for a moment the self that we were long ago when we enter some house or garden in which we used to live in our youth. But these are the most hazardous pilgrimages, which end as often in disappointment as in success. It is in ourselves that we should rather seek to find those fixed places, contemporaneous with different years. And great fatigues followed by a good night's rest can to a certain extent help us to do so. For in order to make us descend into the most subterranean galleries of sleep, fatigue followed by rest will so thoroughly turn over the soil and penetrate the bedrock of our bodies that we discover down there the garden where we played in our childhood. There is no need to travel in order to see it again; we must dig down inwardly to discover it. We shall see how certain fortuitous impressions carry us back to the past, with a more delicate precision, with a more light-winged, more immaterial, more headlong flight than organic dislocations.

On days when, although there was no parade, Saint-Loup had to stay in barracks, I used often to go and visit him there. It was a long way, I had to leave the town and cross the viaduct, from either side of which I had an immense view. A strong breeze blew almost always over this high ground, and swept round the buildings erected on three sides of the barrack square, which howled incessantly like a cave of the winds. While I waited for Robert - he being engaged on some duty or other - outside the door of his room or in the mess, talking to some of his friends to whom he had introduced me (and whom later I came to see from time to time, even when he was not going to be there), looking down from the window at the countryside three hundred feet below me, bare now except where recently sown fields, often still soaked with rain and glittering in the sun, showed a few strips of green, of the brilliance and translucent limpidity of enamel, I often heard him discussed by the others, and I soon learned what a popular favourite he was. Among many of the volunteers, belonging to other squadrons, sons of rich business or professional men who looked at aristocratic high society only from outside and without penetrating its enclosure, the attraction which they naturally felt towards what they knew of Saint-Loup's character was reinforced by the glamour that attached in their eyes to the young man whom, on Saturday evenings, when they went on pass to Paris, they had seen supping in the Cafe de la Paix with the Duc d'Uzes and the Prince d'Orleans. And on that account they associated his handsome face, his casual way of walking and saluting, the jaunty eccentricity of his service dress-with a notion of elegance and tone which, they averred, was lacking in the best turned out officers in the regiment, even the majestic Captain to whom I had been indebted for the privilege of sleeping in barracks, who seemed, in comparison, too pompous and almost common.

On leaving the barracks I would take a stroll and then, to fill up the time before I went, as I did every evening, to dine with Saint-Loup at the hotel in which he and his friends had established their mess, I walked back to my own, as soon as the sun went down, so as to have a couple of hours in which to rest and read.

On the first of these evenings, before we sat down to dinner, I drew Saint Loup into a corner and, in front of all the rest but so that they should not hear me, said to him: "Robert, this is hardly the time or the place for what I am going to say, but I shan't be a second. I keep forgetting to ask you when I'm in the barracks: isn't that Madame de Guermantes photograph that you have on your table?"

"Why yes, she's my dear Aunt"

"Of course she is what a fool I am. I used to know that, but I'd never thought about it. I say your friends will be getting impatient we must be quick, they're looking at us. Or another time will do, it isn't at all important."

"That's alright carry on, they can wait."

"You wouldn't care to give me her photograph, I suppose?"

I had meant to ask him only for the loan of it. But as I was about to speak I was overcome with shyness, feeling that the request was indiscreet, and in order to hide my confusion I formulated it more bluntly and simplified it, as if it had been quite natural.

"No, I should have to ask her permission first." was his answer.

He blushed as he spoke. I could see that he had a reservation in his mind, that he attributed one to me as well, that he would further my love only partially, subject to certain moral principles, and for this I hated him. At the same time I was touched to see how differently Saint-Loup behaved towards me now that I was no longer alone with him, and that his friends formed an audience. His increased affability would have left me cold had I thought it was deliberately assumed, but I could feel that it was spontaneous and simply consisted of all that he was wont to say about me in my absence and refrained as a rule from saying when I was alone with him. True, in our private conversations I could detect the pleasure he found in talking to me, but that pleasure almost always remained unexpressed. Now, at the same remarks of mine which ordinarily he enjoyed without showing it, he watched from the corner of his eye to see whether they produced on his friends the effect on which he had counted and which evidently corresponded to what he had promised them beforehand. The mother of a debutante could be no more anxiously attentive to her daughter's repartee and to the attitude of the audience.

On the third evening, one of his friends, to whom I had not had an opportunity of speaking before, conversed with me at great length; and at one point I overheard him telling Saint-Loup how much he was enjoying himself. And indeed we sat talking together almost the entire evening, leaving our glasses untouched on the table before us, separated from the others by the veils of one of those instinctive likings between men which, when they are not based on physical attraction, are the only kind that is altogether mysterious. Of such an enigmatic nature had seemed to me to be, at Balbec, the feeling which Saint-Loup had for me, a feeling not to be confused with the interest of our conversations, free from any material association, invisible, intangible, and yet of whose presence in himself he had been sufficiently conscious to refer to with a smile. And perhaps there was something more surprising still in this fellow feeling born here in a single evening, like a flower that had blossomed in the warmth of this little room.

I took a particular pleasure in talking to my new friend, as for that matter to all Robert's comrades and to Robert himself, about the barracks, the officers of the garrison, and the Army in general. I had begun to take an interest in the various personalities of the barracks, in the officers whom I saw in the square when I went to visit Saint-Loup, or, if I was awake then, when the regiment passed beneath my windows. I should have liked to know more about the major whom Saint-Loup so greatly admired, and about the course in military history which would have appealed to me "aesthetically". I knew that all too often Robert indulged in a rather hollow verbalism, but at other times gave evidence of the assimilation of profound ideas which he was fully capable of grasping. Unfortunately, in respect of Army matters Robert was chiefly preoccupied at this time with the Dreyfus case. He spoke little about it, since he alone of the party at table was a Dreyfusard. The others were violently opposed to the ideas of a fresh trial, except my other neighbor, my new friend, whose opinions appeared to be somewhat wavering. A firm admirer of the colonel, who was regarded as an exceptionally able officer and had denounced the current agitation against the Army in several of his regimental orders which had earned him the reputation of being an anti-Dreyfusard, my neighbor had heard that his commanding officer had let fall certain remarks leading one to suppose that he had his doubts as to the guilt of Dreyfus and retained his admiration for Picquart.   On this last point at any rate, the rumour of the colonel's relative Dreyfusism was ill-founded, as are all the rumours which float around any great scandal.

22

I did not arrive at Saint-Loup's restaurant every evening in the same state of mind. If a memory, or a sorrow are capable of leaving us, they can also return and sometimes remain with us for a long time. There were evenings when, as I passed through the town on my way to the restaurant, I felt so keen a longing for Mme de Guermantes that I could scarcely breathe; it was as though part of my breast had been cut out and replaced by its equivalent in nostalgia and love. And however neatly the wound may have been stitched together, one lives rather uncomfortably when regret for the loss of another person is substituted for one's entrails. I would look up at the sky. If it was clear, I would say to myself: "Perhaps she is in the country; she's looking at the same stars; and for all I know, when I arrive at the restaurant Robert may say to me: Good news! I've just heard from my aunt. She wants to meet you, she's coming down here."

It was not the firmament alone that I associated with the thought of Mme de Guermantes. A passing breath of air seemed to bring me a message from her, as, long ago, from Gilberte in the wheatfields of Meseglise. One day on entering the dining room I found courage to ask Saint-Loup:

"You don't happen to have had any news from Paris?"

"Yes" he replied gloomily "bad news."

I breathed a sigh of relief when I realised that it was only he who had cause for unhappiness, and that the news was from his mistress. But I soon saw that one of its consequences would be to prevent Robert for a long time from taking me to see his aunt.

I learned that a quarrel had broken out between him and his mistress, through the post presumably, unless she had come down to pay him a flying visit between trains. And the quarrels, even when relatively slight, which they had previously been, had always seemed as though they must prove insoluble. For she had a violent temper, and would stamp her foot and burst into tears for reasons as incomprehensible as those that make children shut themselves into dark cupboards, not come out for dinner, and refuse to give any explanation.

The agony he had experienced during the first few hours at first gave way. What he began to suffer from a little later was a secondary and accidental grief, the tide of which flowed incessantly from within himself, at the idea that perhaps she would be glad to make up, that she was waiting for a word from him, that in the meantime by way of revenge she would, perhaps on a certain evening, do a certain thing, and that he had only to telegraph her that he was coming for it not to happen. Among all these possibilities he was certain of nothing; his mistress preserved a silence which wrought him up to a frenzy of grief.

It has been said that silence is strength; in a quite different sense it is a terrible strength in the hands of those who are loved. It increases the anxiety of the one who waits. Nothing so tempts us to approach another person as what is keeping us apart; and what barrier is so insurmountable as silence?

At length she wrote to ask whether he would forgive her. As soon as he realised that a definite rupture had been avoided he saw all the disadvantages of a reconciliation. Besides, he had already begun to suffer less acutely, and had almost accepted a grief of which, in a few months perhaps, he would have to suffer the sharp bite again if their liaison resumed. He did not hesitate for long. And perhaps he hesitated only because he was now certain of being able to recover. However she asked him, so that she might have time to recover her equanimity, not to come to Paris at the New Year. And he did not have the heart to go to Paris without seeing her.

"I'm sorry about it because of our visit to my aunt, which will have to be put off. I dare say I shall be in Paris at Easter."

I searched all through dinner for a pretext which would enable Saint Loup to ask his aunt to see me without my having to wait. Such pretext was finally furnished by the desire I cherished to see some more pictures by Elstir, the famous painter I had met at Balbec. I was able, during dinner in front of his friends, to say casually, as though on the spur of the moment;

"I say, if you don't mind, just one last word on the subject of the lady we were speaking about. You remember Elstir, the painter?"

"Why of course I do"

"Well one of the reasons I should like to meet the lady is that she has in her house at least one very fine picture by Elstir."

"Really, I never knew that."

"Elstir will probably be at Balbec at Easter, you know he now spends almost the entire year on the coast. I should very much like to have seen this picture before I leave Paris. I don't know whether you're on sufficiently intimate terms with your aunt; but couldn't you manage, somehow, to ask her to let me come and see the picture without you, since you won't be there?"

"Certainly, leave it to me."

One morning, Saint-Loup confessed to me that he had written to my grandmother to give her news of me and to suggest to her that, since there was a telephone service functioning between Paris and Doncieres, she might make use of it to speak to me. In short, that very day she was to give me a call, and he advised me to be at the post office at about a quarter to four. The telephone was not yet at that date as commonly in use as it is today. And yet habit requires so short a time to divest of mystery the sacred forces with which we are in contact that, not having had my call at once, my immediate thought was that it was all very long and very inconvenient, and I almost decided to lodge a complaint. Like all of us nowadays, I found too slow for my linking the admirable sorcery whereby the person to whom we wish to speak finds himself suddenly transported hundreds of miles at the precise moment our fancy has ordained.

That afternoon, alas, at Doncieres, the miracle did not occur. When I reached the post office, my grandmother's call had already been received. At length, I went in search of the telephonist, who told me to wait a while; then I spoke and after a few seconds of silence, suddenly I heard that voice which I mistakenly thought I knew so well; for always until then, every time that my grandmother had talked to me, I had been accustomed to follow what she said on her face, in which the eyes figured so largely; but her voice itself I was hearing this afternoon for the first time. I discovered how sweet that voice was; perhaps indeed it had never been so sweet as it was now, for my grandmother, thinking of me as being far away and unhappy, felt that she might abandon herself to an outpouring of tenderness which she usually restrained and kept hidden. It seemed constantly on the verge of breaking, of expiring in a flow of tears, then too, having it alone beside me, seen without the mask of her face, I noticed in it for the first time the sorrows that had cracked it in the course of a lifetime.

"Granny!" I cried to her "Granny!" and I longed to kiss her, then suddenly I ceased to hear the voice, and was left even more alone. I quivered with the same anguish I had felt when, as a little child, I had lost her in a crowd. An anguish due less to my not finding her than to the thought she must be searching for me, must be saying to herself that I was searching for her, an anguish not unlike that which I was later to feel on the day when we speak to those who can no longer reply and long for them to hear the things we never said. I went on repeating "Granny! Granny!" as Orpheus, left alone, repeats the name of his dead wife. I decided to leave the post office and go find Robert at his restaurant in order to tell him that, as I was half expecting a telegram which would oblige me to return to Paris I wanted, just in case, to know the times of the trains.

When I joined Robert and his friends, I withheld the confession that my heart was no longer with them, that my departure was now irrevocably fixed. Saint-Loup appeared to believe me, but I learned afterwards that he had from the first moment realised that my uncertainty was feigned and he would not see me again next day. While he and his friends, letting their plates grow cold, searched through the time table for a train which would take me to Paris, and while the whistling of the locomotives in the cold starry night could be heard on the line, my departure oppressed me less. I was no longer obliged to think of it alone when I felt the more normal and healthy exertions of my energetic friends, Robert's brothers in arms, were being applied to what was to be done, and of those other strong creatures, the trains, whose comings and goings, morning and night, broke up my long isolation from my grandmother into daily possibilities of return.

The following morning I was late, and failed to catch Saint-Loup, who had already left for the country. I was wretched at having failed to say goodbye, but I went nevertheless, for my only concern was to return to my grandmother. Entering the drawing room I found her there reading. I was in the room, or rather I was not yet in the room since she was not aware of my presence and, like a woman whom one surprises at a piece of needlework she will hurriedly put aside if anyone comes in, she was absorbed in thought. Like a sick man who, not having looked at his own reflection for a long time, recoils on catching sight in the glass, I saw, sitting on the sofa beneath the lamp, red faced heavy and sick, day-dreaming, letting her slightly crazed eyes wander over a book, an overburdened old woman whom I did not know.

23

I found my grandmother not at all well. For some time past, without knowing exactly what was wrong, she had been complaining of her health. It is in sickness we are compelled to recognise that we do not live alone but are chained to a being from a different realm, from whom we are worlds apart, who has no knowledge of us and by whom it is impossible to make ourselves understood: our body. Were we to meet a brigand on the road, we might perhaps succeed in making him sensible of his own personal interest if not of our plight. But to ask pity of our body is like discoursing in front of an octopus, for which our words can have no more meaning than the sound of the tides, and with which we should be appalled to find ourselves condemned to live. My grandmother's ailments often passed unnoticed by her attention, which was always

directed towards us.   When they gave her too much
pain, in the hope of curing them she tried in vain to
understand them. If the morbid phenomena of which
her body was the theatre remained obscure and beyond
the reach of her mind, they were clear and intelligible to
certain beings belonging to the same natural kingdom
as themselves, beings to whom the human mind has
learned gradually to have recourse in order to
understand what its body is saying to it, as when a
foreigner addresses us we try to find someone of his
country who will act as interpreter. These can talk to
our body, can tell us if its anger is serious or will soon be
appeased.

Cottard, who had been called in to examine my
grandmother - and who had infuriated us by asking with
a subtle smile "Ill? You're sure it's not what they call a
diplomatic illness?" tried to soothe his patient's
restlessness by a milk diet. But incessant bowls of milk
soup gave her no relief, because my grandmother
sprinkled them liberally with salt, the injurious effects of
which were then unknown (Widal not yet having made
his discoveries).   For, medicine being a compendium of
the successive and contradictory mistakes of
practitioners, when we summon the wisest of them to
our aid the chances are that we may be relying on a
scientific truth the error of which will be recognised in a
few years' time. So that to believe in medicine would
be the height of folly, if not to believe in it were not a
greater folly still.

Bergotte spoke to me of Dr du Boulbon as a physician
who would discover methods of treatment which,
however strange they might appear, would adapt

themselves, overcome the resistance we put up to them at first, and feed upon rich reserves which were ready made for them without our realising it. I now gave Dr du Boulbon the benefit of that unlimited confidence which is inspired by the man who, with an eye more penetrating than other men's, perceives the truth. I knew indeed that he was more of a specialist in nervous diseases, the man whom Charcot before his death had predicted would reign supreme in neurology and psychiatry. "Ah, I don't know about that. It's quite possible" put in Francoise, who was in the room and was hearing Charcot's name, as indeed du Boulbon's, for the first time. Her "possibles" her "perhapses" her "I don't knows" were peculiarly irritating at such moments. One wanted to say to her: "Naturally you didn't know, since you haven't the faintest idea what we are talking about."

In spite of this more special competence in cerebral and nervous matters, as I knew that du Boulbon was a great physician, I begged my mother to send for him and the hope that, by a clear perception of the malady he might perhaps cure it finally prevailed over the fear that we had that by calling in a consultant we would alarm my grandmother. What decided my mother was the fact that my grandmother no longer went out of doors and scarcely rose from her bed.

Du Boulbon when he came, instead of sounding her chest, gazed at her with his wonderful eyes, in which there was perhaps the illusion that he was making a profound scrutiny of his patient, or the desire to give her that illusion, which seemed spontaneous but must have become mechanical, or not to let her see that he was thinking of something quite different, or to establish his authority over her, and began to talk about Bergotte.

"Ah yes, indeed Madame, he's splendid. How right you are to admire him! But which of his books do you prefer? Oh, really? Why, yes, perhaps that is the best after all. In any case it is the best composed of his novels. Claire is quite charming in it. Which of his male characters appeals to you most?"

I supposed at first that he was making her talk about literature because he found medicine boring, perhaps also to display his breadth of mind and even, with a more therapeutic aim, to restore confidence to his patient, to show her he was not alarmed, to take her mind off the state of her health. But afterwards I realised that he had been seeking to ascertain by these questions whether my grandmother's memory was in good order. With seeming reluctance he began to inquire about her life, fixing her with a stern and sombre eye. Then suddenly, as though he had glimpsed the truth and was determined to reach it at all costs, with a preliminary rubbing of his hands, looking down at my grandmother with a lucid eye, punctuating his words in a quietly impressive tone, he said:

"You will be cured, Madame, on the day, whenever it comes - and it rests entirely with you whether it comes today - on which you realise there is nothing wrong with you and resume your life."

"Your grandmother might perhaps go and sit, if the doctor allows it, in some quiet path in the Champs-Elysees, near that clump of laurels where you used to play when you were little" said my mother to me, thus indirectly consulting Dr du Boulbon and her voice for that reason assuming a tone of timid deference which it would not have had if she had been addressing me alone. The doctor turned to my grandmother and, being a man of letters no less than a man of science, adjured her as follows:

"Go to the Champs-Elysees, Madame, to the clump of laurels which your grandson loves. The laurel will be beneficial to your health. After he had exterminated the serpent Python, it was with a laurel in his hand that Apollo made his entry into Delphi. He sought thus to guard himself from the deadly germs. So you see the laurel is the most ancient, most venerable and, I may add-the most beautiful of antiseptics."

When, after seeing Dr du Boulbon to the door, I returned to the room in which my mother was alone, the anguish suddenly lifted, I sensed that my mother was going to give vent to her joy and would observe mine too, and I tried to speak to Mamma but my voice broke and, bursting into tears, I remained for a long time with my head on her shoulder, weeping, savouring, cherishing my grief, now that I knew it had departed from my life.

Some friends had asked me to meet them next day in the Champs-Elysees, to go with them from there to pay a call together, ending up with a dinner in the country, the thought of which appealed to me. I had no longer any reason to forgo these pleasures. When my grandmother had been told it was now imperative that she should go out as much as possible, she had herself at once suggested the Champs-Elysees. It would be easy for me to escort her there and, while she sat reading, to arrange with my friends where I should meet them later; and I should still be in time, if I made haste, to take the train with them to Ville d'Avray.

When the time came, my grandmother did not want to go out, saying she felt tired. Having obstinately refused to let Mamma stay in the room with her, left to herself she took an endlessly long time over her dressing. Now that I knew she was not ill, with that strange indifference we feel towards our relations so long as they are alive, I thought it very selfish of her to take so long and risk making me late. In my impatience I finally went downstairs without waiting for her. At last she joined me, without apologising to me as she generally did for having kept me waiting, flushed and bothered like a person who has come to a place in a hurry and has forgotten half her belongings. I was startled to see her so flushed, and supposed that having begun by making herself late she had had to hurry over her dressing.

When we left the cab at the corner of the Avenue Gabriel, in the Champs-Elysees, I saw my grandmother turn away without a word and make for the little old pavilion with its green trellis at the door of which I had once waited for Francoise. I expected her to begin "I'm afraid I've kept you waiting; I hope you'll still be in time for your friends" but she did not utter a single word, so much so that, feeling a little hurt, I was disinclined to speak first. Finally, looking up at her I noticed that as she walked beside me she kept her face turned the other way. I was afraid she might be feeling sick again. I looked at her more closely and was struck by

177

her gait. Her hat was crooked, her cloak stained; she had the disheveled appearance of a person who has just been knocked down by a carriage or pulled out of a ditch.

"I was afraid you were feeling sick, Grandmamma?"

I guessed rather than heard what she said, so inaudible was the voice in which she mumbled.

"Come!" I said lightly enough not to seem to be taking her illness too seriously "since you're feeling a little sick I suggest we go home"

"I didn't like to suggest it because of your friends" she replied "Poor pet! But if you don't mind, I think it would be wiser."

I was afraid of her noticing the strange way in which she uttered these words.

"Come" I said to her brusquely "you mustn't tire yourself talking when you're feeling sick - it's silly; wait till we get home."

She smiled at me sorrowfully and gripped my hand. She had realised there was no need to hide from me what I had guessed, that she had had a slight stroke.

24

We made our way back along the Avenue Gabriel through the strolling crowds. I left my grandmother to rest on a bench and went in search of a cab. She, in whose heart I always placed myself, was now closed to me, had become part of the external world, and I was obliged to keep from her what I thought, to betray no sign of my anxiety. She had suddenly returned to me the thoughts, the griefs which, from my earliest childhood, I had entrusted to her for all time. She was not yet dead, but I was already alone.

The sun was sinking; it burnished an interminable wall along which our cab had to pass before reaching the street in which we lived, a wall against which the shadow of horse and carriage cast by the setting sun stood out in black on a ruddy background, like a hearse

179

on some Pompeian terra-cotta. At length we arrived at the house. I sat the invalid down at the foot of the staircase in the hall and went up to warn my mother. As soon as I began to speak, my mother's face was convulsed by a despair which was yet already so resigned that I realised she had been holding herself quietly in readiness.

The trouble affected my grandmother's eyes. For some days she could not see at all. Her eyes were not like those of a blind person, but remained just the same as before. I gathered that she could see nothing only from the strangeness of a certain smile of welcome which she assumed the moment one opened the door, until one had come up to her and taken her hand, a smile which began too soon and remained stereotype on her lips, fixed but always full-faced, and endeavouring to be visible from every quarter, because it could no longer rely on the eyes to regulate it, to indicate the right moment to focus it, to make it vary according to the change of position of the person who had come in. Because it was left isolated it assumed in its awkwardness an undue importance, giving an impression of exaggerated amiability. Then her sight was completely restored, and from her eyes the wandering affliction passed to her ears. For several days my grandmother was deaf. And as she was afraid of being taken by surprise by someone she would not have heard, all day long she kept turning her head sharply towards the door.

Her pain grew less, but the impediment in her speech increased. We were obliged to ask her to repeat almost everything. And now my grandmother, realising that we could no longer understand her, gave up the attempt and lay still. When she caught sight of me she gave a sort of convulsive start, but could make no intelligible sound. Then, overcome by her sheer powerlessness, she let her head fall back on the pillows, stretched herself out flat on her bed, her face grave and stony, her hands motionless on the sheet or occupied in some purely mechanical action such as that of wiping her fingers with her handkerchief. She made no effort to think. Then came a state of perpetual agitation. She was incessantly trying to get up. We restrained her so far as we could from doing so, for fear of her discovering how paralysed she was. One day when she had been left alone for a moment I found her out of bed, standing in her nightdress trying to open the window.

The doctor gave my grandmother an injection of morphine, and ordered cylinders of oxygen. My mother, the doctor, the nursing sister held these in their hands; as soon as one was exhausted another was put in its place. I had left the room for a few minutes. When I returned I found myself in the presence of a sort of miracle. Accompanied by an incessant low murmur, my grandmother seemed to be singing us a long joyous song which filled the room, rapid and musical. Perhaps to a slight extent it reflected some improvement brought about by the morphine. Principally it was the result of a change in the register of her breathing. Released by the twofold action of the oxygen and the morphine my grandmother's breath no longer laboured, no longer whined, but glided like a skater. Perhaps the breath, imperceptible as that of the wind in the hollow stem of a reed, was mingled in this song with some of those more human signs which, released at the approach of death, suggest intimations of pain or happiness in those who have already ceased to feel.

When my lips touched her face, my grandmother's hands quivered, and a long shudder ran through her whole body - a reflex, perhaps, or perhaps it is that certain forms of tenderness have, so to speak, a hyperaesthesia which recognises through the veil of unconsciousness what they scarcely need senses to enable them to love. Suddenly my grandmother half rose, made a violent effort like someone struggling to resist an attempt on his life. Francoise could not withstand this sight and burst out sobbing. Remembering what the doctor had said I tried to make her leave the room. At that moment my grandmother opened her eyes. I thrust myself hurriedly in front of Francoise to hide her tears, while my parents were speaking to the patient. The hiss of oxygen ceased; the doctor moved away from the bedside. My grandmother was dead.

An hour later Francoise was able for the last time, and without causing any pain, to comb that beautiful hair which was only tinged with grey and hitherto had seemed less old than my grandmother herself. But now, on the contrary, it alone set the crown of age on a face grown young again, from which had vanished the wrinkles, contractions, swellings, the strains which pain had carved on it over the years. As in the days when her parents had chosen for her a groom, she had the features, delicately traced by purity and submission, the cheeks glowing with a chaste expectation, a dream of happiness, and innocent gaiety even, which the years had gradually destroyed. Life in withdrawing from her had taken with it the disillusionments. A smile seemed to be hovering on my grandmother's lips. On that funeral couch death, like a sculptor of the Middle Ages, had laid her down in the form of a young girl.

25

Although it was simply a Sunday in autumn, I had been born again, life lay intact before me, for that morning, after a succession of mild days, there had been a cold fog which had not cleared until nearly midday: and a change in the weather is sufficient to create the world and ourselves anew. Formerly, when the wind howled in my chimney, I would listen to the blows which it struck on the iron trap with as keen an emotion as if, like the famous chords with which the Fifth Symphony opens, they had been the irresistible calls of a mysterious destiny. Every change in the aspect of nature offers us a transformation by adapting our desires to the new form of things. The mist, from the moment of my awakening, had made of me, instead of the centrifugal being which one is on fine days, a man turned in on himself, longing for the chimney corner and the shared bed, a shivering Adam in quest of a sedentary Eve, in this different world.

Between the soft grey tint of a morning landscape and the taste of a cup of chocolate I incorporated all the originality of the physical, intellectual and moral life which I had taken with me to Doncieres about a year earlier and which, blazoned with the oblong form of a bare hillside - always present even when it was invisible - formed in me a series of pleasures entirely distinct from all others in the sense that the impressions which orchestrated them were a great deal more characteristic of them to my unconscious mind than any facts I might have related. From this point of view the new world in which this morning's fog had immersed me was a world already known to me (which only made it more real) and forgotten for some time (which restored all its novelty). And I was able to look at several of the pictures of misty landscapes which my memory had acquired, notably a series of "Mornings at Doncieres" including my first morning there in barracks and another in a neighboring country house where I had gone with Saint-Loup to spend the night, from the windows of which, when I had drawn back the curtains at daybreak before getting back into bed, in the first a trooper, in the second (on the thin margin of a pond and a wood, all the rest of which was engulfed in the uniform and liquid softness of the mist) a coachman busy polishing harness, had appeared to me like those figures which emerge from a faded fresco.

It was from my bed that I was contemplating these memories that afternoon, for I had returned to it to wait until the hour came at which, taking advantage of the absence of my parents who had gone for a few days to Combray, I proposed to get up and go to a little play which was being given that evening in Mme de Villeparisis's drawing room. Had they been at home I should perhaps not have ventured to do so; my mother, in the delicacy of her respect for my grandmother's memory, wished the tokens of regret that were paid to it to be freely and sincerely given; she would not have forbidden me this outing, but she would have disapproved.

Suddenly, although I had heard no bell, Francoise opened the door to introduce Albertine, who entered smiling, silent, plump, containing in the plenitude of her body the days we spent together in that Balbec to which I had never since returned. No doubt, whenever we see again a person with whom our relations - however trivial they may be- have now changed, it is a juxtaposition of two different periods. For this, there is no need for a former mistress to call round to see us as a friend; all that is required is the visit of someone we have known in a certain kind of life, and that this life should have ceased for us. On each of Albertine's features I could read the question: "Well, well, there are no cliffs here, but you don't mind if I sit down beside you all the same, as I used to do at Balbec?" She was an enchantress offering me a mirror that reflected time. In this she resembled all the people whom we seldom see now but with whom at one time we lived on more intimate terms. With Albertine, however, there was something more. True, even in our daily encounters at Balbec, I had always been surprised, so changeable was her appearance. But now she was scarcely recognisable. Freed from the pink haze that shrouded them, her features had emerged in sharp relief like those of a statue. She had another face, or rather she had a face at last; her body too had grown. There remained scarcely anything now of the sheath in which she had been enclosed and on the surface of which, at Balbec, her future outline had been barely visible.

This time, Albertine had returned to Paris earlier than usual. As a rule she did not arrive until the spring so that I did not distinguish, in the pleasure that I felt, the return of Albertine from that of the fine weather. It was enough I should be told she was in Paris and that she had called at my house for me to see her again like a rose flowering by the sea. I cannot say whether it was the desire for Balbec or for her that took possession of me then; perhaps my desire for her was itself a lazy, cowardly and incomplete form of possessing Balbec, as if to possess a thing materially were tantamount to possessing it spiritually. Contrary to the habitual order of her holiday movements, this year she had come straight from Balbec, where furthermore she had not stayed nearly so late as usual. It was a long time since I had seen her and I knew nothing of her life during the periods in which she abstained from coming to see me. Then, one fine day, in would burst Albertine, whose rosy apparitions and silent visits left me little if any better informed as to what she might have been doing during an interval which remained plunged in that darkness of her hidden life. This time, however, certain signs seemed to indicate that some new experience must have entered into that life. And yet, perhaps, all one was entitled to conclude from them was that girls change very rapidly at the age Albertine had reached.

In any case, whatever the modifications that might perhaps have explained why it was she now so readily accorded to my momentary and purely physical desire what at Balbec she had refused with horror to allow to my love, an even more surprising one manifested itself in Albertine that same evening as soon as her caresses had procured in me the satisfaction she could not fail to notice and which, indeed, I had been afraid might provoke in her the instinctive movement of offended modesty Gilberte had made at a similar moment behind the laurel shrubbery in the Champs-Elysees.

The exact opposite happened. Already, when I had first made her lie on my bed and had begun to fondle her, Albertine had assumed an air which I did not remember in her, of docile good will. Obliterating every trace of her customary pretensions, the moment preceding pleasure, similar in this respect to the moment that follows death, had restored to her rejuvenated features what seemed like the innocence of childhood. No doubt everyone whose special talent is suddenly brought into play becomes modest, diligent and charming; especially if by this talent such persons know they are giving us pleasure, are themselves made happy by it and want us to enjoy it to the full. But in this new expression on Albertine's face there was more than generosity, there was a sort of conventional and unexpected zeal.

Albertine seemed to feel it would indicate a certain coarseness on her part were she to think this material pleasure could be unaccompanied by a moral sentiment. She, who had been in a great hurry, now, doubtless because she felt that kisses implied love and love took precedence, seemed embarrassed at the idea of getting up and going immediately after what had happened. I insisted on her going home and finally she did go, but she was so ashamed on my account at my discourtesy that she laughed almost as though to apologize for me, as a hostess to whose party you have gone without dressing makes the best of you but is offended nevertheless.

Albertine had made me so late that the play had just finished when I entered Mme de Villeparisis's drawing room; and having little desire to be caught in the stream of guests who were pouring out, discussing the great piece of news (the separation, which was said to have been already effected, between the Duc de Guermantes and his wife) I had taken a seat on a bergère in the outer room while waiting for an opportunity to greet my hostess, when from the inner one, where she had no doubt been sitting in the front row, I saw emerging; majestic, ample and tall in a flowing gown of yellow satin, the Duchess herself. The sight of her no longer disturbed me. One fine day, my mother, laying her hands on my forehead and saying "You really must stop hanging about trying to meet Mme de Guermantes. You're becoming a laughing-stock. You really have more to think about than waylaying a woman who doesn't care a straw about you" instantaneously - like a hypnotist who brings you back from the distant country in which you imagined yourself to be, and opens your eyes for you, had awakened me from an unduly protracted dream; and then it was over. I had given up my morning walks, and with so little difficulty I thought myself justified in the prophecy (which we shall see was to prove false) that I should easily grow accustomed, during the course of my life, to no longer seeing a woman.

But it had never occurred to me that my recovery, in restoring me to a normal attitude towards Mme de Guermantes, would have a corresponding effect on her and make possible a friendliness, even a friendship, which no longer mattered to me. Until then, the efforts of the entire world banded together to bring me into touch with her would have been powerless to counteract the evil spell cast by an ill-starred love. In such cases nothing can avail us until the day we utter sincerely in our hearts the formula: "I am no longer in love." I had been vexed with Saint-Loup for not having taken me to see his aunt, but he was no more capable than anyone else of breaking a spell. An absence, the declining of an invitation, an unintentional, unconscious harshness are of more service than all the cosmetics and fine clothes in the world. There would be plenty of social success if people were taught upon these lines.

As she swept through the room, the Duchess caught sight of me on my bergère, genuinely indifferent and seeking only to be polite, whereas while I was in love I had tried so desperately, without ever succeeding, to assume an air of indifference. She swerved aside, came towards me, reproducing the smile she had worn that evening at the Opera. "No, don't move" she said, gracefully gathering in her immense skirt. "You don't mind if I sit beside you a moment?"

She was taller than me, and further enlarged by the volume of her dress, and I felt myself almost touching her bare arm, round which a faint down exhaled as if it were a perpetual golden mist, and the blonde coils of her hair wafted their fragrance over me. Having barely room to sit down, she could not turn easily to face me, and so assumed the sort of soft and dreamy expression one sees in a portrait.

"Have you any news of Robert?" she inquired.

At that moment Mme de Villeparisis entered the room.

"Well what a fine time you arrive when we do see you here for once!"

And noticing that I was talking to her niece, and concluding, perhaps, that we were more intimate than she had supposed: "But don't let me interrupt your conversation with Oriane" she went on (for the good offices of the procuress are part of the duties of the perfect hostess) "You wouldn't care to dine with her here on Wednesday?"

It was the day on which I was to dine with Mme de Stermaria, so I declined.

"Saturday, then?"

As my mother was returning Saturday, it would have been unkind. I therefore declined this invitation also.

"Ah, you're not an easy person to get hold of."

"Why do you never come to see me?" inquired Mme de Guermantes when Mme de Villeparisis had left us to go and congratulate the performers. "It's such a bore never to see each other except in other people's houses. Since you won't dine with me at my aunt's, why not come and dine at my house?"

Various people who were at last preparing to leave, seeing that the Duchess had sat down to talk to a young man on a seat so narrow as just to contain them both, thought they must have been misinformed, that it was not the Duchess but the Duke who was seeking a separation, on my account. They hastened to spread this intelligence. I had better grounds than anyone for being aware of its falsity. But I was surprised that at one of those difficult periods in a separation the Duchess, instead of withdrawing from society, should go out of her way to invite a person whom she knew so slightly. The suspicion crossed my mind that it had been the Duke alone who had been opposed to having me in the house, and that now she saw no further obstacle to surrounding herself with the people she liked.

"You wouldn't be free on Friday, now, for a small dinner party? It would be so nice. There'll be the Princesse de Parme, who's charming, not that I'd ask you to meet anyone who wasn't agreeable."

I must admit that a surprise of a different sort was to follow the one I had on hearing Mme de Guermantes ask me to dine with her.

"You know I'm the aunt of Robert de Saint-Loup who is very fond of you" In replying that I was aware of this I added that I also knew M de Charlus, "who had been very kind to me at Balbec and in Paris." Mme de Guermantes appeared surprised and her eyes seemed to turn, as though for verification, to some much earlier page of her internal register. "What, so you know

Palamède, do you?" This name took on a considerable charm on the lips of Mme de Guermantes because of the instinctive simplicity with which she spoke of a man who was socially so brilliant but for her was no more than her brother in law and the cousin with whom she had grown up.

"You must admit he's odd and - though it's not very nice of me to say such a thing about a brother in law I'm devoted to - a trifle mad at times. But, are you absolutely sure you're not thinking of someone else? Do you really mean my brother in law Palamède? I know he loves mystery, but this seems a bit much."

I replied that I was absolutely sure.

"Well, I must leave you" said Mme de Guermantes, as though with regret.

I have to look in for a moment at the Princesse de Ligne's. You aren't going on there? No? You don't care for parties? You're very wise, they're too boring for words. If only I didn't have to go! But she's my cousin; it wouldn't be polite. I'm sorry, for my own sake, because I could have taken you there, and brought you back after, too. Good-bye then; I look forward to seeing you on Friday."

26

About two months after my dinner with the Duchess and while she was at Cannes, having opened an envelope the appearance of which had not led me to suppose it contained anything out of the ordinary, I read the following words: "The Princesse de Guermantes, *nee* Duchesse en Baviere, At Home, the — -th." No doubt to be invited to the Princesse de Guermantes's was perhaps not, from the social point of view, any more difficult than to dine with the Duchess. But my imagination, like Elstir engaged upon rendering some effect of perspective without reference to the notions of physics which he might well possess, depicted for me not what I knew but what it saw. How, in any case, could it be otherwise? We are bored at the dinner table because our imagination is absent, and because it is keeping us company we are interested in a book. The fact remains these differences do exist, people are never completely alike. Among the characteristics peculiar to the Princesse de Guermantes' salon, the one most generally cited was an exclusiveness due in part to the Princess's royal birth but more especially to the almost fossilised rigidity of the Prince's aristocratic prejudices which, incidentally, the Duke and Duchess had no hesitation deriding in front of me. This exclusiveness made me regard it as even more improbable I should have been invited by this man who reckoned only in royal personages and dukes and at every dinner party made a scene because he had not been put in the place to which he would have been entitled under Louis XIV, a place which, thanks to his immense erudition in matters of history and genealogy, he was the only person who knew. For this reason, many society people came down on the side of the Duke and Duchess when discussing the differences that distinguished them from their cousins. "The Duke and Duchess are far more modern, far more intelligent, they aren't simply interested, like the other couple, in how many quarterings one has, their salon is three hundred years in advance of their cousins' were customary remarks, the memory of which made me tremble as I looked at the invitation card.

The day on which the reception at the Princesse de Guermantes was to be held, I learned that the Duke and Duchess had returned to Paris and I made up my mind to go see them that morning. It was the Duke alone who received me in his library. I asked him if he thought there was any chance of my seeing Mme de Stermaria at the Princess's.

"Why no" he replied with the air of a connoisseur. "I know the name you mention, from having seen it in club directories, it isn't at all the type of person who goes to Gilbert's. You'll see nobody there who is not excessively well bred and intensely boring, duchesses bearing titles one thought were extinct years ago, all the ambassadors, foreign royalties, but you mustn't expect even the ghost of a Stermaria. Gilbert would be taken ill at the mere thought of such a thing. Wait now, you're fond of painting, I must show you a superb picture I bought from my cousin, partly in exchange for the Elstirs, which frankly didn't appeal to us. It was sold to me as a Philippe de Champaigne, but I believe myself it's by someone even greater. Would you like to know what I think? I think it's a Velazquez, and of the best period," said the Duke, looking me boldly in the eyes, either to ascertain my impression or in the hope of enhancing it. A footman came in.

"Mme la Duchesse wishes to know if M le Duc will be so good as to see M Swann, as Mme la Duchesse is not quite ready."

"Show M Swann in" said the Duke, after looking at his watch and seeing that he still had a few minutes before he need go to dress. "Naturally my wife, who told him to come, isn't ready. No point in saying anything in front of Swann about Marie-Gilbert's party" said the Duke "I don't know whether he's been invited. Gilbert likes him immensely, because he believes him to be the natural grandson of the Duc de Berry, but that's a long story. You can imagine - my cousin, who has a fit if he sees a Jew a mile off. But now of course the Dreyfus case has made things more serious. Swann ought to have realised that he more than anyone must drop all connection with those fellows, instead of which he says the most regrettable things."

I had not seen Swann for a long time, and found myself wondering momentarily whether in the old days he used to clip his moustache, or whether his hair had not been *en brosse,* for I found him somehow changed. He was indeed greatly changed because he was very ill. Swann was dressed with an elegance which, like that of his wife, associated with what he now was what he once had been. Buttoned up in a pearl-grey frock-coat which emphasised his tall, slim figure, his white gloves stitched in black, he had a grey topper of a flared shape which Delion no longer made except for him, the Prince de Sagan, M de Charlus and Comte Louis de Turenne. I was surprised at the charming smile and affectionate handclasp with which he replied to my greeting for I had imagined that after so long he would not recognise me; I told him of my astonishment; he received it with a shout of laughter, a trace of indignation and a further squeeze of my hand, as if it were to throw doubt on the soundness of his brain or the sincerity of his affection to suppose he did not recognise me. And yet that was in fact the case; he did not identify me, as I learned long afterwards, until several minutes later when he heard my name mentioned. But no change in his face, his speech, in the things he said to me betrayed the discovery which a chance word from M de Guermantes had enabled him to make, with such absolute sureness did he play the social game. He brought to it, moreover, that spontaneity in manners and that personal enterprise, even in matters of dress, which characterised the Guermantes style. Thus the greeting which the old clubman had given me without recognising me was not the cold, stiff greeting of the purely formalist man of the world, but a greeting full of real friendliness, genuine charm, such as the Duchesse de Guermantes possessed.

"Now, Charles, you're a great expert, come and see what I've got to show you, after which I'm going to leave you together for a moment while I go and change my clothes. Besides, I expect Oriane won't be long now." And he showed his "Velazquez" to Swann. "But it seems to me I know this" said Swann with the grimace of a sick man for whom the mere act of speaking requires an effort.

"Yes" said the Duke, perturbed by the time which the expert was taking to express his admiration. "You've probably seen it at Gilbert's."

"Oh yes, of course, I remember."

"What do you suppose of it?"

"Oh, well, if it comes from Gilbert's house it's probably one of your ancestors," said Swann with a blend of irony and deference towards a grandeur which he would have felt it impolite to belittle, but to which he preferred to make only a playful reference.

"Of course it is" said the Duke bluntly. "I've heard the names of Rigaud, Mignard, even Velazquez mentioned" he went on, fastening on Swann the look of an inquisitor in an attempt at once to read his mind and to influence his response. "Well, do you think it's by one of those big guns I've mentioned?"

"Nnnnno," Swann hesitated for a moment in front of the picture, which he obviously thought atrocious.

The Duke could not restrain an impulse of rage. When this had subsided: "Be good fellows, both of you, wait a moment for Oriane, I must go and put on my swallow-tails and then I'll be back. I shall send word to the missus that you're both waiting for her."

I chatted for a minute or two with Swann about the Dreyfus case and asked him how it was that all the Guermantes were anti-Dreyfusards. "In the first place because at heart all these people are anti-semites" replied Swann, who nevertheless knew very well that certain of them were not but, like everyone who holds a strong opinion, preferred to explain the fact that other people did not share it by imputing to them prejudices against which there was nothing to be done, rather than reasons which might permit of discussion.

"Yes it's true I've been told that the Prince de Guermantes is anti-semitic."

"Oh that fellow! I don't even bother to consider him. He carries it to such a point that when he was in the army and had a toothache he preferred to bear it rather than go to the only dentist in the district, who happened to be a Jew, and later on he allowed a wing of his castle to be burned to the ground because he would have had to send for extinguishers to the place next door, which belongs to the Rothschilds."

"Are you going to be there this evening, by any chance?"

"Yes" Swann replied "although I don't really feel up to it. But he sent me a wire to tell me that he has something to say to me. I feel I shall soon be too unwell to receive him at my house, so I prefer to get it over at once."

"But the Duc is not anti-semitic?"

"You can see quite well that he is, since he's an anti-Dreyfusard" replied Swann, without noticing that he was begging the question. "All the same I'm sorry to have disappointed the fellow - His Grace I should say - by not admiring his Mignard or whatever he calls it."

M de Guermantes returned and was presently joined by his wife, all ready now for the evening, tall and proud in a gown of red satin the skirt of which was bordered with sequins. She had in her hair a long ostrich feather dyed purple, and over her shoulders a tulle scarf of the same red as her dress. "How nice it is to have one's hat lined in green" said the Duchess, who missed nothing. "However with you, Charles, everything is always charming, whether it's what you wear or what you say, what you read or what you do." Swann meanwhile, without apparently listening, was considering the Duchess as he would have studied the canvas of a master, and then sought her eyes, making a face which implied the exclamation "Gosh!" Mme de Guermantes rippled with laughter. "So my clothes please you? I'm delighted. But I must say they don't please me much" she went on with a sulky air. "God what a bore it is to have to dress up and go out when one would ever so much rather stay at home!"

"What magnificent rubies!"

"Ah! My dear Charles, at least one can see that you know what you're talking about, you're not like that brute Monserfeuil who asked me if they were real. I must say I've never seen anything quite like them. They were a present from the Grand Duchess. They're a little too big for my liking, a little too like claret glasses filled to the brim, but I've put them on because we shall be seeing the Grand Duchess this evening at Marie-Gilbert's" added Mme de Guermantes, never suspecting that this assertion destroyed the force of those previously made by the Duke.

"What's on at the Princess's?" inquired Swann.

"Practically nothing," the Duke hastened to reply, the question having made him think Swann was not invited.

"What do you mean, Basin? The whole world has been invited. It will be a deathly crush. What will be pretty, though," she went on, looking soulfully at Swann, "if the storm I can feel in the air now doesn't break, will be those marvelous gardens. You know them, of course. I was there a month ago, when the lilacs were in flower. You can't imagine how lovely they were. And then the fountain - really it's Versailles in Paris. And that reminds me, Charles, of what I was going to say to you when you were telling me about your San Giorgio of Venice. We have a plan, Basin and I, to spend next spring in Italy and Sicily. If you were to come with us, just think what a difference it would make! I'm not thinking only of the pleasure of seeing you, but imagine, after all you've told me about the remains of the Norman Conquest and of antiquity, imagine what a trip like that would become if you were with us! I mean to say that even Basin - what am I saying, Gilbert! - would benefit by it, because I feel that even his claims to the throne of Naples and all that sort of thing would interest me if they were explained by you in old Romanesque churches in little villages perched on hills."

"Madame, I'm very much afraid that it won't be possible."

"Indeed! Mme de Montmorency is more fortunate. You went with her to Venice and Vicenza. She told me that with you one saw things one would never see otherwise, things no one had ever thought of mentioning before, that you showed her things she'd never dreamed of, and that even in the well-known things she was able to appreciate details she might have passed without noticing. She's certainly been more highly favoured than we are to be."

Swann burst out laughing.

"I should like to know, all the same," Mme de Guermantes asked him, "how you can tell ten months in advance that a thing will be impossible."

"My dear Duchess I'll tell you if you insist but, first of all, you can see I'm very ill."

"Yes, my Charles, I don't think you look at all well. I'm not pleased with your colour. But I'm not asking you to come with us next week. In ten months one has time to get oneself cured, you know."

At this point a footman came in to say the carriage was at the door. "Come, Oriane," said the Duke, already pawing the ground with impatience as though he were himself one of the horses that stood waiting outside.

"Very well, give me in one word the reason you can't come to Italy" the Duchess put it to Swann as she rose to say good-bye to us.

"But my dear lady, it's because I shall have been dead for several months. According to the doctors the thing I've got - which may carry me off an any moment - won't in any case leave me more than three or four months to live, and even that is a generous estimate," replied Swann with a smile, while the footman opened the glazed door of the hall to let the Duchess out.

"What's that you say?" cried the Duchess, stopping for a moment on her way to the carriage and raising her beautiful, melancholy blue eyes, now clouded by uncertainty. Placed for the first time in her life between two duties as incompatible as getting into her carriage to go out to dinner and showing compassion for a man who was about to die, she could find nothing in the code of conventions that indicated the right line; not knowing which to choose, she felt obliged to pretend not to believe the latter, in order to comply with the first, which at the moment demanded less effort, and thought the best way of settling the conflict would be to deny that any existed. "You're joking" she said to Swann.

"It would be a joke in charming taste," he replied. "I don't know why I'm telling you this. I've never said a word to you about my illness before. But since you asked me, and since now I may die at any moment...But whatever I do I mustn't make you late; you're dining

203

out, remember," he added, because he knew that for other people their social obligations took precedence over the death of a friend.

"Come, Oriane, don't stop there chattering like that with Swann; you know Mme de Saint-Euverte insists on sitting down at eight sharp. Forgive me Charles" he went on, turning to Swann, "but it's ten minutes to eight already."

Mme de Guermantes advanced resolutely towards the carriage and uttered a last farewell to Swann. "You know, we'll talk about that another time; I don't believe a word you've been saying, but we must discuss it quietly. I expect they've frightened you unnecessarily. Come to lunch, any day you like" and, lifting her red skirt, she set her foot on the step. She was just getting into the carriage when the Duke cried out "Oriane, what have you been thinking? You've kept on your black shoes! With a red dress! Go upstairs and put on red shoes or rather," he said to the footman, "Tell Mme la Duchesse's maid at once to bring down a pair of red shoes."

"But my dear," replied the Duchess gently, embarrassed to see that Swann, who was leaving the house with me but had stood back to allow the carriage to pass out in front of us, had heard, "seeing that we're late…"

"No, no, we have plenty of time. They'll wait for us, but you can't possibly go there in a red dress and black shoes. Besides, we shan't be the last; the Sassenages are coming and you know they never arrive before twenty to nine."

The Duchess went up to her room.

"Well," said M de Guermantes to Swann and myself, "people laugh at us poor husbands, but we have our uses. But for me Oriane would have gone to dinner in black shoes. Good bye, my boys," he said, thrusting us gently from the door, "off you go before Oriane comes down again. If she finds you still here she'll start talking again. She's already tired and she'll reach the dinner-table quite dead. Besides, I tell you frankly, I'm dying of hunger. I had a wretched lunch this morning. Five minutes to eight! Ah, women! Now, don't let yourself be alarmed by those damned doctors, they're fools. You'll bury us all."

27 - CITIES OF THE PLAIN

My second arrival at Balbec was very different from the first. The manager had come in person to meet me at Pont-a-Coulevre, reiterating how greatly he valued his titled patrons, which made me afraid he had ennobled me until I realised that, in the obscurity of his grammatical memory, *titre* meant simple *attitre*, or accredited. The more new languages he learned the worse he spoke the others. He brought me a message from Albertine. She had not been due to come to Balbec that year but, having changed her plans, had been for the last three days ten minutes away by train. She sent word now to ask when I could see her. I inquired whether she had called in person. "Yes," replied the manager. "She would like it to be as soon as possible." But for my part, I wished to see nobody. On my arrival, I had been seized once again by the indolent charm of seaside existence. As I traveled through what had formerly been a strange hotel, this time I had the soothing pleasure of passing through a hotel that I knew, where I felt at home, where I had performed that operation which consists in the imposition of our own familiar soul on the terrifying soul of our surroundings.

Next day I went, at Mamma's request, to lie down for a while on the beach, or rather among the dunes, where one is hidden by their folds, and where I knew that Albertine and her friends would not be able to find me. My drooping eyelids allowed but one kind of light to pass, entirely pink, the light of the inner walls of the eyes. Then they shut altogether, whereupon my grandmother appeared to me, seated in an armchair. So feeble was she that she seemed to be less alive than other people, and yet I could hear her breathe; now and again she made a sign to show that she had understood what we were saying, my father and I. But in vain did I take her in my arms, I could not kindle a spark of affection in her eyes, a flush of color in her cheeks. A few days later I was able to look with pleasure at the photograph Saint-Loup had taken of her. The photograph showed her looking so elegant, so carefree, beneath the hat which partly hid her face, that I saw her as less unhappy and in better health than I had supposed.

Then one day I decided to send word to Albertine that I would see her. This was because, on a morning of intense and premature heat, the cries of children at play, of bathers, of newsvendors, had traced for me in interlacing flashes the scorching beach which the little waves came up to sprinkle; then the concert mingled

207

with the lapping of the surf, through which violins hummed like a swarm of bees that had strayed out over the sea. At once I longed to hear Albertine's laughter and to see her friends again, silhouetted against the waves. But on the day on which Albertine came the weather had turned dull and cold again, and I had no opportunity of hearing her laugh; she was in a very bad mood. "Balbec is deadly dull this year," she said to me. "I don't mean to stay any longer than I can help. You know I've been here since Easter, that's more than a month. There's not a soul here. You can imagine what fun it is."

Notwithstanding the recent rain and a sky that changed every moment, after escorting Albertine as far as Epreville, I went off by myself in the direction of the high road that Mme de Villeparisis's carriage used to take when we went for drives with my grandmother; pools of water, which the sun, now bright again, had not yet dried, made a regular quagmire of the ground, and I thought of my grandmother who could never walk a yard without covering herself in mud. But on reaching the road I found a dazzling spectacle. Where I had seen with my grandmother in August only the green leaves of the apple trees, as far as the eye could reach they were in full bloom, unbelievably luxuriant, their feet in the mire beneath their ball-dresses, heedless of spoiling the marvelous pink satin, which glittered in the sunlight; the distant horizon of the sea gave the trees the background of a Japanese print; if I raised my head to gaze at the sky through the flowers, which made its serene blue appear almost violent, they seemed to draw apart to reveal the immensity of their paradise. Beneath that azure a faint but cold breeze set the blushing bouquets gently trembling. Blue-tits came and perched upon the branches and fluttered among the indulgent flowers. Then the rays of the sun gave place suddenly to those of rain; they streaked the whole horizon, enclosing the line of apple-trees in their grey net. But these continued to hold aloft their pink and blossoming beauty, in the wind that had turned icy beneath the drenching rain: it was a day in Spring.

My grief for my grandmother's death was diminishing. Although I was still incapable of feeling a renewal of physical desire, Albertine was beginning nevertheless to inspire in me a desire for happiness. I would gladly have postponed its realisation until the following winter, without seeking to see Albertine again at Balbec before her departure. But, even in the midst of a grief that is still acute, physical desire will revive. It would be untrue, I think, to say that there were already symptoms of that painful mistrust which Albertine was to inspire in me, not to mention that special character which the mistrust was to assume. The incident did not occur until some weeks later. It arose out of a remark made by Cottard.

On the day in question Albertine and her friends had wanted to drag me to the casino at Incarville where I would not have joined them (wanting to pay a visit to Mme Verdurin who had invited me several times), had I not been held up at Incarville itself by a train breakdown. As I strolled up and down waiting for the men to finish working at it, I found myself all of a sudden face to face with Dr Cottard, who had come to see a patient. I made him come with me to the little casino, one that had struck me as gloomy on the evening of my first arrival, now filled with the tumult of the girls who, in the absence of male partners, were dancing together. I remarked to Cottard how well they danced. He, taking the professional point of view of a doctor and with an ill-breeding which overlooked the fact they were my friends, replied: "Yes, but parents are very rash to allow their daughters to form such habits. I should certainly never let mine come here. There, now, look" he went on, pointing to Albertine and Andrée who were waltzing slowly, tightly clasped together "I've left my glasses behind and can't see very well, but they are certainly keenly roused. It's not sufficiently known that women derive most excitement through their breasts. And theirs, as you can see, are touching completely." And indeed the contact between the breasts of Andrée and of Albertine had been constant. I do not know whether they heard or guessed Cottard's observation, but they drew slightly apart while continuing to waltz. At that moment Andrée said something to Albertine, who laughed with the same deep and penetrating laugh I had heard before, but the unease it roused in me this time was painful. Albertine appeared to be conveying, to making Andrée share, some secret and voluptuous thrill.

28

The mischief his remarks about Albertine and Andrée
had done me was extreme, but its worst effects were
not immediately felt, as happens with forms of
poisoning which begin to act only after a time. From
the day when Cottard accompanied me into the casino
Albertine seemed to me different; the sight of her made
me angry. I myself had changed, quite as much as she
had changed in my eyes. I had ceased to wish her well;
to her face, behind her back when there was a chance
of my words being repeated to her, I spoke of her in the
most wounding terms.

One day, outside the Grand Hotel, I had just been
addressing Albertine in the harshest, most humiliating
language, and in order to make my attitude still more
marked, to say all the nicest possible things to

Andrée. As soon as we were alone and had moved along the corridor, Albertine began: "What have you got against me?" Before answering her, I escorted her to the door of my room.   Opening it, I went across to the window; the gulls had settled upon the waves; I drew Albertine's attention to them. "Don't change the subject" she said, "be frank with me." I lied. I told her she must listen to a confession, that of a great passion I had for Andrée. I made this confession with a simplicity and frankness worthy of the stage, but seldom expressed in real life except in declaring a love which one does not feel. I went so far (in order to make her more ready to believe me) as to let fall the admission that at one time I had been on the point of falling in love with her, but that she was no more to me now than a good friend.

As it happened, in underlining to Albertine these protestations of coldness towards her I was merely accentuating more markedly that binary rhythm which love adopts in all those who have too little confidence in themselves to believe a woman can ever fall in love with them, and they can genuinely fall in love with her. They know themselves well enough to have observed that in the presence of the most divergent types of woman they felt the same hopes, the same agonies, invented the same romances, uttered the same words. Their sense of their own instability increases their misgivings that this woman, by whom they so long to be loved, does not love them. Why should chance have brought it about, when she is simply an accident placed in the path of our surging desires, that we should ourselves be the object of the desires that she feels?

This fear and shame provoke the counter rhythm by first drawing back, to resume the offensive and regain respect and domination; the rhythm is perceptible in the various periods of a single love affair, in all the corresponding periods of similar love affairs, in all those people whose self-analysis outweighs their self esteem.

This avowal to Albertine of an imaginary sentiment for Andrée enabled me at length, without any danger that Albertine might interpret it as love, to speak to her with a tenderness which I had so long denied myself and which seemed to me exquisite. As I spoke to her of her friend whom I loved, tears came to my eyes. She looked so sweet, so wistfully docile, as though her whole happiness depended on me, that I could barely restrain myself from kissing this new face which seemed to have melted into pure goodness. I was moved to pity at the sight of this sweet girl, accustomed to being treated in a friendly and loyal fashion, whom the good friend that she might have supposed me to be had been pursuing for weeks past. It was because I placed myself at a standpoint that was purely human, external to both of us, from which my jealous love had evaporated, that I felt for Albertine that pity which would have been less profound if I had not loved her. When we count up afterwards the sum of all we have done for a woman, we often discover that the actions prompted by the desire to show we love her bulk scarcely larger than those due to the human need to repair the wrongs we do, from a mere sense of moral duty.

I finally made bold to tell her what had been reported to me about her way of life, and said that notwithstanding the disgust I felt for women tainted with that vice, I had not given it a thought until I had been told the name of her accomplice, and that she could readily understand, loving Andrée as I did, the pain this had caused me. The terrible revelation that Cottard had made to me had struck home.

Albertine, even before swearing to me that it was not true, expressed, like everyone upon learning that things are being said about them, anger, concern, and, with regard to the slanderer, a fierce curiosity to know who he was. But she assured me that she bore me no resentment.

"If it had been true I would have told you. But Andrée and I both loathe that sort of thing. We haven't reached our age without seeing women with cropped hair who behave like men and do the things you mean, and nothing revolts us more."

Albertine merely gave me her word, unsupported by proof. But this was precisely what was best to calm me. It is the property of love to make us at once more distrustful and more credulous. We must be in love before we can care that all women are not virtuous, and we must be in love too before we can hope that some are. Statements that are capable of relieving us seem all too readily true.

Doubtless I had long been conditioned, by the powerful impression made on my imagination and my faculty for emotion by the example of Swann, to believe in the truth of what I feared rather than of what I should have wished. Hence the comfort brought me by Albertine's affirmations came near to being jeopardized for a moment because I remembered the story of Odette.

But I told myself that, if it was right to allow for the worst when trying to understand Swann's sufferings, I must nevertheless not end up regarding one supposition as more true than the rest because it was the most painful. Was there not a vast gulf between Albertine and Odette, a whore sold by her mother in her childhood? There could be no comparison. Albertine had in no sense the same interest in lying to me that Odette had in lying to Swann.

I had before me a new Albertine - whom I had already, it was true - a frank, kind Albertine who, out of affection for myself had just forgiven my suspicions and tried to dispel them. She made me sit by her side on my bed. I thanked her, assuring her that our reconciliation was complete, and that I would never be harsh to her again.

29 - THE FUGITIVE

At daybreak, my face still turned to the wall, and before I had seen above the big window curtains what shade of colour the first streaks of light assumed, I could already tell what the weather was like.   The first sounds from the street told me, according to whether they came to my ears deadened by the atmosphere or quivering like arrows in the empty expanses of a frosty morning. As soon as I heard the first tramcar I could tell whether it was sodden with rain or setting forth into the blue. It was, in fact, principally from my bedroom that I took in the life of the outer world during this period.

I would ring for Francoise. I would open the *Figaro*. I would scan its columns and ascertain that it did not contain an article which I had sent to the editor, which was no more than a revised version of the page written long ago in Dr Percepied's carriage, as I gazed at the spires of Martinville. Then I would read Mamma's letter. She found it odd, if not shocking, that a girl should be living with me. On the first day, at the moment of leaving Balbec, when she saw how wretched I was and was worried about leaving me by myself, my mother had perhaps been glad when she heard that Albertine was traveling with us. But if at the start my mother had not been hostile to this proposal, she had become so, now that it had been completely realised and the girl was prolonging her sojourn in our house, moreover in the absence of my parents. I cannot however say that my mother ever openly manifested this hostility to me. As in the past, when she had ceased to reproach me with my nervous instability and my laziness, now she had qualms - which perhaps I did not altogether perceive or did not wish to perceive at the time - about running the risk, by offering any criticism of the girl to whom I had told her that I intended to make an offer of marriage, of casting a shadow over my life, of sowing perhaps, for a season when she herself would no longer be there, the seeds of remorse at having grieved her by marrying Albertine.

However all this may be, and apart from any question of propriety, I doubt whether Mamma could have put up with Albertine, since she had habits of punctuality and order of which my mistress had not the remotest conception. She would never think of shutting a door and, by the same token, would no more hesitate to enter a room than would a dog or a cat. Her somewhat inconvenient charm was, in fact, that of behaving in the household not so much like a girl as like a domestic animal which comes into a room and goes out again, and is to be found wherever one least expects. She would often - something that I found profoundly restful

- come and lie down beside me on my bed, making a place for herself from which she never stirred, without disturbing me as a person would have done.

Without feeling to the slightest degree in love with Albertine, without including in the list of my pleasures the moments that we spent together, I had nevertheless remained preoccupied with the way in which she disposed of her time; had I not fled from Balbec in order to make certain she could no longer meet this or that person with whom I was afraid of her doing wrong? And Albertine had such extraordinary passivity, such a powerful faculty for complying with wishes, that these relations had indeed been severed and the phobia that haunted me cured. But such a phobia is capable of assuming as many forms as the undefined evil that is its cause. So long as my jealousy had not been reincarnated in new people, I had enjoyed after the passing of my anguish an interval of calm. But the slightest pretext serves to revive a chronic disease.

30

On certain fine days, the weather was so cold, one was in such full communication with the street, that it seemed as though the outer walls of the house had been dismantled, and whenever a tramcar passed, the sound of its bell reverberated like a silver knife striking a house of glass. But it was above all in myself that I heard, with rapture, a new sound emitted by the violin within, its strings tautened or relaxed by differences in temperature or light. Within our being, an instrument which the uniformity of habit has rendered mute, song is born of these variations, the source of all music; the change of weather on certain days makes us pass at once from one note to another. These modifications alone, internal though they had come from without, gave me a fresh vision of the external world.

Communicating doors, long barred, reopened in my brain. The life of certain towns, the gaiety of certain excursions, resumed their place in my consciousness. With my whole being quivering around the vibrating string, I would have sacrificed my dim former existence and my life to come, erased by habit, for a state so unique.

Then, like a famished convalescent already battening upon all the dishes that are still forbidden him, I wondered whether marriage with Albertine might not spoil my life, not only by making me assume the task of devoting myself to another person, but by forcing me to live apart from myself because of her continual presence and depriving me for ever of the joys of solitude.

And not of these alone. Of Albertine, I had nothing more to learn. Every day she seemed to me less pretty. Only the desire that she aroused in others raised her in my eyes to a lofty pinnacle. She was capable of causing me pain, but no longer joy. Pain alone kept my wearisome attachment alive. I was miserable at the thought this state of affairs should persist and, at certain moments, I longed to hear of something terrible she had done, something that would keep us estranged.

Jealousy is one of those intermittent maladies the cause of which is capricious, arbitrary, always identical in the same patient, sometimes entirely different in another. There are asthma sufferers who can assuage their attacks by opening the windows, inhaling the pure air of mountains, others by taking refuge in a smoke filled room. There are few men whose jealousy does not allow certain derogations. One will consent to infidelity provided he is told of it, another provided it is concealed from him, wherein they are equally absurd, since if the latter is more literally deceived inasmuch as the truth is not disclosed, the other demands from that truth the aliment, the extension, the renewal of his sufferings.

When we used to go to dinner at La Raspeliere, she went to great lengths to ensure that I should have no cause for jealousy. I remembered I had known a different Albertine then all at once she had changed into another; the Albertine of today.   And for this change I could hold no one responsible but myself. Everything she would have admitted to me readily when we were simply good friends had ceased to flow from her as soon as she suspected I was in love with her, or had divined the existence in me of a sentiment that desires to know, yet suffered from knowing and seeks to learn still more. Ever since that day she had concealed everything from me. She kept away from my room whether she thought my visitor was male or female, she whose eyes used at one time to sparkle so brightly whenever I mentioned a girl: "You must try and get her to come here. I'd be amused to meet her." "But she's what you call a bad type." "Precisely, that'll make it all the more fun." At that moment, I might perhaps have learned all there was to know. And even when, in the little Casino, she had withdrawn her breasts from Andrée's, I believe this was due not to my presence but to that of Cottard, who was capable of giving her a bad reputation.

Our engagement was assuming the aspect of a criminal trial, and gave her the timorousness of a guilty party. Now she changed the conversation whenever it turned on people, men or women, who were not of mature years. It was when she had not yet suspected that I was jealous of her that I should have asked her to tell me what I wanted to know. One ought always to take advantage of that period. It is then one's mistress tells one about her pleasures and even the means by which she conceals them.

Love, I used to say to myself, is what we feel for a person; jealousy seems directed towards that person's actions. We feel that if she were to tell us everything, we might perhaps be cured of our love. However skillfully jealousy is concealed by him who suffers it, it is very soon detected by her who has inspired it. She seeks to put us off the scent of what might make us unhappy, and easily succeeds, for to the man who is not forewarned, how should a casual remark reveal the falsehoods that lie beneath it?

No doubt, in the first days at Balbec, Albertine seemed to exist on a parallel plane to that on which I was living, but one that had converged on it (after my visit to Elstir) and had finally joined it, as my relations with her, at Balbec, in Paris, then at Balbec again, grew more intimate. Sometimes, when I got up to fetch a book from my father's study, my mistress was so tired after her long outing in the morning and afternoon in the open air that when I returned I found her asleep. Stretched out at full length on my bed, in an attitude so natural no art could have devised it, she reminded me of a long blossoming stem that had been laid there; and so in a sense she was; the faculty of dreaming, which I possessed only in her absence, I recovered at such moment in her presence, as though by falling asleep she had become a plant. In this way, her sleep realised to a certain extent the possibility of love; alone, I could think of her, but I missed her, I did not possess her; when she was present I spoke to her, but was too absent from myself to be able to think of her. When she was asleep, I no longer had to talk, I knew I was no longer observed by her, I no longer needed to live on the surface of myself.

By shutting her eyes, by losing consciousness, Albertine stripped off, one after another, the different human personalities with which she had deceived me. I had an impression of possessing her entirely which I never had when she was awake. Her life submitted to me, exhaled towards me its gentle breath. I listened to this murmuring, soft as a sea breeze, magical as a gleam of moonlight, that was her sleep. So long as it lasted, I was free to dream about her and yet at the same time to look at her and, when that sleep grew deeper, to kiss her. What I felt then was a love as pure as nature. And indeed her sleep, a delight of which I never tired, was to me a whole landscape. Her sleep brought within my reach something as serene, as sensual as those nights of full moon on the bay of Balbec calm as a lake over which the branches barely stir, where, stretched out upon the sand, one could listen for hours on end to the surf breaking and receding. I spent many a charming evening talking and playing with Albertine, but none so sweet as when I was watching her sleep.

But this pleasure of seeing her sleep, which was as sweet to me as that of feeling her live, was cut short by another pleasure, that of seeing her wake. It was gratifying to me that when, from the underworld of sleep, she climbed the last steps of the staircase of dreams, it was in my room that she was reborn to consciousness and life, that she wondered for an instant: "Where am I?" In that first delicious moment of uncertainty, it seemed to me that once again I was taking possession of her completely since, instead of her returning to her own room after an outing it was my room that was about to enclose her without there being any misgiving in her eyes, which remained as calm as if she had never slept at all. Then she would find her tongue and say: "My darling Marcel." After this she pursed her lips in a little pout which spontaneously transformed into a kiss. As quickly as she had earlier fallen asleep, she had awoken.

There was blended, in my need to keep Albertine every evening by my side, something that had hitherto been foreign to my amorous existence, if it was not entirely new in my life. It was a soothing power the like of which I had not experienced since the evenings at Combray long ago when my mother, stooping over my bed, brought me repose in a kiss. To be sure, I should have been greatly astonished at that time had anyone told me that I was not extremely kind and especially that I would ever seek to deprive someone else of a pleasure. I must have known myself imperfectly then, for my pleasure in having Albertine live with me was less a positive pleasure than the pleasure of withholding joy from others. To love carnally was, for me, to enjoy a triumph over rivals. I can never repeat it often enough: it was more than anything else an appeasement.

Suffering, when we are in love, ceases from time to time, only to resume in a different form. We weep to see the beloved no longer respond to us with burst of affection, we suffer even more when, having relinquished them with us, she resumes them with others; then from this suffering, we are distracted by a new and still more agonising pang, the suspicion she has lied to us. This suspicion is in turn dispelled, and we are soothed by our mistress's affectionate kindness; but then we observe an air of boredom, longing, melancholy while we are talking. We observe like a black sky the slovenly clothes she puts on when she is with us, keeping for other people the dresses with which she used to flatter us. If, on the contrary, she is affectionate, what a joy for a moment! Then the feeling she is bored by us returns. But suddenly this pain is reduced to nothing when we think of where she has been, where she still goes perhaps during the hours we are not with her, those places in which she is separated from us, does not belong to us, is happier than when she is with us. Such are the revolving searchlights of jealousy.

It was no longer the peace of my mother's kiss at Combray that I felt when I was with Albertine on these evenings, but on the contrary the anguish of those on which my mother scarcely bade me good-night, or even did not come up to my room at all because she was kept downstairs by guests. As soon as she was a captive in my house, the bird I had seen one afternoon advancing with measured tread along the front, surrounded by a congregation of other girls like seagulls, Albertine had lost all her colours, together with all the opportunities that other people had of securing her for themselves. Gradually she had lost her beauty. Shame, jealousy, the memory of my first desires and of the brilliant setting, had restored to Albertine her former beauty and worth. And thus there alternated with the somewhat oppressive boredom I felt in her company a throbbing desire, full of resplendent images and of regret, according to whether she was by my side in my room or I set her free again in my memory. Every person we love, indeed to a certain extent every person, is to us like Janus, presenting to us a face that pleases us if the person leaves us, a dreary face if we know him or her to be at our disposal.

31

I learned that a death occurred which distressed me
greatly - that of Bergotte. It was known that he had
been ill for a long time past. Not, of course, with the
illness from which he had suffered originally and which
was natural. Nature scarcely seems capable of giving us
any but quite short illnesses, but medicine has
developed the art of prolonging them. The
circumstances of his death were as follows. A fairly mild
attack of uraemia had led to his being ordered to
rest. But, an art critic having written somewhere that in
Vermeer's *View of Delft* (lent by the Gallery at the
Hague for an exhibition of Dutch painting), a picture
which he adored and imagined that he knew by heart, a
little patch of yellow wall, which he could not
remember, was so well painted that it was, if one
looked at it by itself, like some priceless specimen of

Chinese art, of a beauty that was sufficient in itself, Bergotte ate a few potatoes, left the house, and went to the exhibition. At the first few steps he had to climb, he was overcome by an attack of dizziness. He walked past several pictures and was struck by the aridity and pointlessness of such an artificial kind of art, which was greatly inferior to the sunshine of a windswept Venetian palazzo, or of an ordinary house by the sea. At last he came to the Vermeer which he remembered as different from anything else he knew, but in which, thanks to the critic's article, he noticed for the first time some small figures in blue, that the sand was pink, and finally the precious substance of the tiny patch of yellow wall. His dizziness increased; he fixed his gaze, like a child upon a yellow butterfly it wants to catch, on the precious little patch of wall. "That's how I ought to have written" he said "My books are too dry, I ought to have gone over them with a few layers of colour, made my language precious in itself, like this little patch of yellow wall." Meanwhile he was not unconscious of the gravity of his condition.   He repeated to himself "Little patch of yellow wall, sloping roof, little patch of yellow wall." Meanwhile he sank down on to a circular settee; whereupon he suddenly ceased to think that his life was in jeopardy and, reverting to his natural optimism, told himself: "It's nothing, a touch of indigestion from those potatoes, which were undercooked." He rolled down from the settee to the floor, as visitors came hurrying. He was dead.

They buried him, but all through that night of mourning, in the lighted shop-windows, his books, arranged three by three, kept vigil like angels with outspread wings and seemed, for him who was no more, the symbol of his resurrection.

I learned, as I have said, that Bergotte had died that day. And I was amazed at the inaccuracy of the newspapers which - each of them - stated he had died the day before. For Albertine had met him, she informed me that evening, and had been late in coming home, for he had chatted to her for some time...

I should then have known that Albertine was lying but a strange darkness clouded my mind. Swann's death had deeply distressed me at the time. We talk of "death" for convenience, but there are almost as many deaths as there are people. We do not possess a sense that would enable us to see, moving at speed in every direction, these deaths aimed by destiny at this person or that. They come in haste, then depart to attend to other tasks. And it is this diversity of deaths, the mystery of their circuits, the color of their fatal badge, that makes so moving a paragraph in the newspapers as this:

"We learn with deep regret that M Charles Swann passed away yesterday at his residence in Paris after a long and painful illness. A Parisian whose wit was widely appreciated, a discriminating but steadfastly loyal friend, he will be universally mourned, not only in those literary and artistic circles where the rare discernment of his taste made him a willing and welcome guest, but also at the Jockey Club of which he was one of the oldest and most respected members."

Swann was a remarkable intellectual and artistic personality, and although he had "produced" nothing, still he was lucky enough to survive a little longer. My dear Charles Swann, whom I used to know when I was still so young and you were nearing your grave, it is because he whom you must have regarded as a young idiot has made you the hero of his novel that your name will perhaps live.

I must also add (and this is what for a long time made Swann's death more painful) that countless questions occurred to me which I longed to ask him about the most disparate subjects: Vermeer, Swann himself, a Boucher tapestry, Combray - questions which were doubtless not very urgent since I had put off asking them from day to day, but which seemed to me of cardinal importance now that no answer would ever come. The death of others is like a journey one might oneself make, when already sixty miles out of Paris one remembers one has left two dozen handkerchiefs behind, forgotten to leave a key with the cook, to say good bye to one's uncle, to ask the name of the town where the old fountain is that you want to see.

32

Albertine had never told me that she suspected me of being jealous. The only words we had exchanged - fairly long ago, it must be said - on the subject of jealousy seemed to prove the opposite. At La Raspeliere, when M de Charlus had made a display of friendly gallantry towards Albertine, I had said to her: "Well he gave you a good hug." And added half ironically: "I suffered all the torments of jealousy." Albertine replied "What a kidder you are! I know quite well you're not jealous. It's perfectly obvious, get along with you!"

She had never told me since then that she had changed her mind; but she must have formed a number of fresh ideas on the subject, for that evening when, on reaching home, after going to fetch her from her own room and taking her to mine, I said to her (with a certain awkwardness which I did not myself understand, for I had indeed told Albertine that I was going to pay a call and had said I did not know where) "Guess where I've been - at the Verdurins'" I had barely had time to utter the words before Albertine, a look of utter consternation on her face, had answered me in words which seemed to explode of their own accord with a force which she was unable to contain: "I thought as much."

"I didn't know you'd be annoyed by my going to see the Verdurins." (It is true she had not told me she was annoyed, but it was obvious. It is true also that I had not said to myself she would be annoyed. And yet, faced with the explosion of her wrath, it seemed to me I could never have expected anything else.)

"Annoyed? What difference does it make to me? I couldn't care less. Wasn't Mlle Vinteuil to be there?"

"You never told me you'd met her the other day," I said to her, to show her I was better informed than she knew.

"Did I meet her?"

"Besides," I said to her angrily "there are plenty of other things you hide from me, such as for instance when you went for three days to Balbec." I smiled with the air of a man who knows far more than he is prepared to say: "But that's only one thing out of hundreds. For instance, only this evening, at the Verdurins, I learned that what you had told me about Mlle Vinteuil..."

Albertine gazed at me fixedly with a tormented air, seeking to read in my eyes how much I knew. Now, what I knew and what I was about to tell her was the truth about Mlle Vinteuil. It is true that it was not at the Verdurins that I had learned it, but long ago. But since I had always refrained, deliberately, from mentioning it to Albertine, I could now appear to have learned it only this evening. It had been all very well for Albertine to tell me that her relations with Mlle Vinteuil and her friend had been perfectly pure, but how could she, when I swore to her (without lying) that I knew the habits of these two women, how could she maintain any longer that, having lived in daily intimacy with them, she had not been the object of approaches on their part which would have made her break with them, if on the contrary she had not acquiesced? But I had no time to tell her what I knew. Albertine, imagining that I had learned the truth either from Mlle Vinteuil, if she had been at the Verdurins, or simply from Mme Verdurin herself, who might have mentioned her to Mlle Vinteuil, did not allow me the chance to speak but made a confession.

"When I lie to you, it's always out of affection for you. And it needed this fatal Verdurin party to open your eyes to the truth, which perhaps they exaggerated a bit, incidentally."

"But why?"

"Because it's dreadfully vulgar, I'd be ashamed to say such a thing in front of you."

Alas! Albertine was several persons in one. But while she was speaking there continued within me, in that curiously alive and creative sleep of the unconscious, the quest for what she had meant. And so, just as she was telling me that she had never felt so affronted as when she had heard that I had gone out alone, my unconscious parallel search for what she had meant to say had come to fruition, and the despair into which my discovery plunged me could not be completely hidden, so that instead of defending, I accused myself. "My little Albertine," I said to her in a gentle voice which was drowned in my first tears, "I could tell you that you're mistaken, that what I did this evening was nothing, but I should be lying; it's you who are right, you have realised the truth, my poor sweet, which is that six months ago, three months ago, when I was still so fond of you, I should never have done such a thing. It's a mere nothing, and yet it's enormous, because of the immense change in my heart of which it is the sign. And since you have detected this change which I hoped to conceal from you, I feel impelled to say this to you: My little Albertine" (I went on in a tone of profound gentleness and sorrow) "don't you see that the life you're leading here is boring for you. It is better that we should part, and as the best partings are those that are effected most swiftly, I ask you, to cut short the great sorrow that I am bound to feel, to say good-bye to me tonight and to leave in the morning without my seeing you again, while I'm asleep."

She appeared stunned, incredulous: "Tomorrow? You really mean it?"

"We have been happy together, but now we feel that we should be unhappy."

"Don't say that we feel that we'd be unhappy" Albertine interrupted me, "don't say 'we', it's only you who feel that."

234

"Yes, very well, you or I, as you like, for one reason or another. But it's absurdly late, you must go to bed - we've decided to part."

"Excuse me, *you've* decided, and I obey you because I don't want to upset you."

"Very well, it's I who have decided, but that doesn't make it any less painful for me. I don't say it will be painful for long, but for the first few days I shall be so miserable without you. And so I feel that it's no use stirring up the memory with letters, we must end everything at once."

"Yes, you're right" she said to me with a crushed air, which was enhanced by signs of fatigue on her features, "rather than have one finger chopped off and then another, I prefer to lay my head on the block at once."

"Heavens, I'm appalled when I think how late I'm keeping you out of bed, it's madness. However, it's the last night! You'll have plenty of time to sleep for the rest of your life. It hurts me terribly to have to leave you."

"It hurts me a thousand times more." replied Albertine.

I had tears in my eyes, like those people who, alone in their rooms, imagining, in the wayward course of their meditations, the death of someone they love, conjure up so precise a picture of the grief they would feel that they end by feeling it. There was only one moment when I felt a kind of hatred for her, which merely sharpened my need to hold on to her.

From morning till night, I never ceased to grieve over Albertine's departure. Set free once more, released from the cage here at home, Albertine had regained all her attraction in my eyes; she had become once more the girl whom everyone pursued, the marvelous bird of the earliest days.

33

I forsook all pride with regard to Albertine, and sent her
a despairing telegram begging her to return on any
terms, telling her that she could do whatever she liked,
that I asked only to be allowed to take her in my arms
for a minute three times a week, before she went to
bed. And if she had said once a week only, I would have
accepted.

She never came back. My telegram had just gone off to
her when I myself received one. It was from Mme
Bontemps. "My poor friend, our little Albertine is no
more. Forgive me for breaking this terrible news to you
who were so fond of her. She was thrown from her
horse against a tree while she was out riding. If only I
had died in her stead!"

Instinctively I drew my hand over my throat, over my lips, which felt themselves kissed by her lips still after she had gone away, and would never be kissed by them again; I drew my hand over them, as Mamma had caressed me at the time of my grandmother's death, saying to me "My poor boy, your grandmother who was so fond of you will never kiss you again." All my life to come seemed to have been wrenched from my heart. My life to come? Had I not, then, thought at times of living it without Albertine? Of course not! Had I then for a long time past pledged her every minute of my life until my death? I had indeed! This future indissolubly blended with hers was something I had never had the vision to perceive, but now that it had been demolished, I could feel the place it occupied in my gaping heart.

Francoise, who still knew nothing, came into my room. In a sudden fury I shouted at her: "What do you want?" Then she said to me: "Monsieur has no need to look cross. In fact he's going to be pleased. Here are two letters from Mademoiselle Albertine."

I must have stared at her with the eyes of a man whose mind has become unhinged. Albertine's two letters must have been written shortly before the fatal ride. The second contained only these words:

"Is it too late for me to return to you? Would you be prepared to take me back? I shall abide by your decision, but I beg you not to be long in making it known; you can imagine how impatiently I shall be waiting. If it is to tell me to return, I shall take the train at once. Yours with all my heart, Albertine."

So then my life was entirely altered. What had constituted its sweetness - not because of Albertine, but concurrently with her, when I was alone - was precisely the perpetual resurgence, at the bidding of identical moments, of moments from the past. From the sound of pattering raindrops I recaptured the scent of the lilacs at Combray; from the shifting of the sun's rays on the balcony the pigeons in the Champs-Elysees; from the muffling of sounds in the heat of morning, the cool taste of cherries; the longing for Brittany or Venice from the noise of the wind and the return of Easter. Tomorrow, the day after, it was a prospect of life together, perhaps for ever, that was opening up; my heart leapt towards it, but it was no longer there. Albertine was dead.

How could she have seemed dead to me when now, in order to think of her, I had at my disposal those same images which I used to recall when she was alive? Either swift-moving and bent over the wheel of her bicycle, strapped on rainy days inside the warrior tunic of her waterproof which moulded her breasts, her head turbaned and dressed with snakes, when she spread terror through the streets of Balbec; or else on the evening when we had taken champagne into the woods of Chantepie, her voice provocative and altered, her face suffused with warm pallor, reddened only on the cheekbones, and when, unable to make it out in the darkness of the carriage, I drew her into the moonlight in order to see it more clearly, the face I was now trying in vain to recapture, to see again in a darkness that would never end. A little statuette on the drive to the island in the Bois, a still and plump face with coarse grained skin at the pianola, she was thus by turns rain-soaked and swift, provoking and diaphanous, motionless and smiling, an angel of music. In this way each one was attached to a moment, to the date of which I found myself carried back when I saw again that particular Albertine. And these moments of the past do not remain still; they retain in our memory the motion which drew them towards the future - towards a future which has itself become the past.

34

"Oh, it's too incredible" said my mother. "You know at my age one has ceased to be astonished at anything, but I assure you that nothing could be more unexpected than the news I've just read in this letter."

"Well," I replied, "I don't know what it is, but however astonishing it may be, it can't be quite so astonishing as what I've learnt from mine. It's a marriage. Robert de Saint-Loup is marrying Gilberte Swann."

And my mother smiled at me with that faint trace of emotion which, ever since she had lost her own mother, she felt at every event that concerned human creatures who were capable of grief and recollection and who themselves also mourned their dead. And so my mother smiled at me and spoke to me in a gentle voice, as though she were afraid, by treating this marriage lightly, of belittling the melancholy feelings it might arouse in Swann's widow and daughter, in Robert's mother who had resigned herself to being parted from her son, all of whom Mamma, in her kindness of heart, in her gratitude for their kindness to me, endowed with her own faculty of maternal emotion.

"Can you imagine for a moment," my mother said to me, "what old Swann - not that you ever knew him, of course - would have felt if he could have known that one day a great grandchild would mingle with the blood of the Duc de Guise!"

"But you know, Mamma, it's more surprising than that. Because the Swanns were respectable people and, given the social position their son acquired, his daughter might have married very well indeed. But everything had to start again from scratch because he married a whore."

"Oh, a whore, you know, people were perhaps rather malicious. I never quite believed it all."

This engagement was to provoke keen comment in the most different social circles. Several of my mother's friends, who had met Saint-Loup in our house, came to her and inquired whether the bridegroom was indeed the same person as my friend. People in society who had taken no notice of Gilberte said to me with an air of solemn interest: "Ah! She's the one who's marrying the Marquis de Saint-Loup" and studied her with the attentive gaze of people who relish the social gossip of Paris.

I saw a good deal of Gilberte at this time, as it happened. Let a certain period of time elapse, and you will see friendships renewed between the same persons as before, after long years of interruption, with pleasure. After ten years the reasons which made one party love too passionately - the other unable to endure - no longer exist. The affinity alone survives, and everything Gilberte would have refused me in the past, that had seemed to her intolerable, she granted me quite readily - doubtless because I no longer desired it. Although neither of us had ever mentioned the reason for this change, if she was always ready to come to me, never in a hurry to leave me, it was because the obstacle had vanished; my love.

35 - TIME REGAINED

I should have no occasion to dwell upon this visit I paid to Combray had it not brought me at least a provisional confirmation of certain ideas I had conceived along the Guermantes way and the Meseglise way. Because of the heat, and also because Gilberte spent the afternoon painting, we did not go out for our walk until about two hours before dinner. The pleasure of those earlier walks, the crimson sky mirroring itself in the Vivonne, was now replaced by nightfall, when one encountered nothing in the village but the blue-grey irregular and shifting triangle of a flock of sheep being driven home. Over one half of the fields the sun had set; above the other half the moon was alight and would soon bathe them. It sometimes happened that Gilberte let me go without her, and I set off trailing my shadow behind me like a boat gliding. But as a rule Gilberte came with me. The walks we took thus were often those I used to take as a child; how then could I help but feel the conviction I would never be able to write, reinforced by the conviction my imagination had weakened, when I found how incurious I was about Combray? I found the Vivonne narrow and ugly. Separated as I was by a lifetime from places I happened to be passing through again, I was saddened by the thought that my faculty of feeling things must have diminished since I no longer took pleasure in these walks. Gilberte herself, who understood me even less than I understood myself, increased my melancholy by sharing my astonishment. "What," she would say, "you feel no excitement when you turn into this little footpath which you used to climb?" and she herself had changed so much that I no longer thought she was beautiful at all. As we walked we chatted - very agreeably for me. Not without difficulty, however. In so many people there are different strata which are not alike; Gilberte was like one of those countries with which one dare not form an alliance because of their frequent changes of government. I remember that, in the course of these walks, on several occasions she surprised me a great deal. The first time was when she said to me: "If you were not too hungry and if it was not so late, by taking that road to the left in less than a quarter of an hour we should be at Guermantes." It was as though she had said to me: "Turn to the left and you will touch the intangible". One of my other surprises was that of seeing the "source of the Vivonne," which I imagined as something as extra terrestrial as the Gates of Hell, and which was merely a sort of rectangular basin in which bubbles rose. And the third occasion was when Gilberte said to me: "If you like, we might after all go out one afternoon and then we can go to Guermantes, taking the road by Meseglise, which is the nicest way," a sentence which upset all the ideas of my childhood by informing me the two "ways" were not irreconcilable. But what struck me most forcibly was how little, during this stay, I relived my childhood years, how little I desired to see Combray, how narrow and ugly I thought the Vivonne.   But where Gilberte corroborated some of my childhood imaginings along the Meseglise way was during one of those walks which were more or less nocturnal - for she dined so late. Before descending into the mystery of a deep and flawless valley carpeted with moonlight, we stopped for a moment like two insects about to plunge into a flower. Opening my heart suddenly with a tenderness born of the fragrant evening breeze, I said to her: "You were speaking the other day of the little footpath. How I loved you then!" She replied: "Why didn't you tell me? I had no idea. I loved you too. In fact I flung myself twice at your head." "When?" "The first time at Tansonville. You were going for a walk with your family, and I was on my way home, I'd never seen such a pretty little boy. I was in the habit," she went on with a vaguely bashful air, "of going to play with boys I knew in the ruins of the keep of Roussainville. And you will tell me that I was a very naughty girl, for there were girls and boys there of all sorts who took advantage of the darkness. I can't tell you how I longed for you to come there too; I remember quite well that, as I had only a moment in which to make you understand what I wanted, I signaled to you so vulgarly that I'm ashamed of it to this day. But you stared at me so crossly that I saw you didn't want to." And suddenly I thought to

246

myself that the true Gilberte, the true Albertine, were perhaps those who had at the first moment yielded themselves with their eyes, one through the hedge of pink hawthorn, the other on the beach. And it was I who, having been incapable of understanding this, having failed to recapture the impression until much later in my memory after an interval in which a dividing hedge of sentiment had made them afraid to be as frank, had ruined everything.

"And the second time," Gilberte went on, "was years later when I passed you in the doorway of your house, the day before I met you again at my aunt Oriane's. I didn't recognise you at first, or rather I did unconsciously recognise you because I felt the same attraction I had at Tansonville."

"But in the meantime there's been the Champs-Elysees."

"Yes, but there you were too fond of me. I felt you were prying into everything I did."

"Moreover," Gilberte went on, "even on the day when I passed you in the doorway, you were still just the same as at Combray; if you only knew how little you'd changed!"

I pictured Gilberte again in my memory. I could have drawn the rectangle of light which the sun cast through the hawthorns, the spade the little girl was holding in her hand, the slow gaze she fastened on me. Only I had supposed that it was a contemptuous gaze because what I longed for it to mean seemed to be a thing little girls did not know about and did only in my imagination, during my hours of solitary desire. Still less could I have supposed that so casually, almost under the eyes of my grandfather, one of them would have had the audacity to suggest it.

And so I was obliged, after so many years, to touch up a picture which I recalled so well - an operation which made me quite happy. I felt a stab of desire and regret when I thought of the dungeons of Roussainville. And yet I was glad to be able to tell myself the pleasure towards which I used to strain every nerve in those days had indeed existed elsewhere than in my mind. In short, the image of Gilberte summed up everything I had desired in my walks to the point of seeming to see the tree trunks part asunder and take human form. She had been ready, if only I had been able to understand. More completely than I had supposed, Gilberte had been in those days truly part of the Meseglise way.

"All that is a long time ago," she said to me, "I've never given a thought to anyone but Robert since the day of our engagement. And even so, you see, it's not those childish whims I feel most guilty about."

All day long, in that slightly too countrified house which seemed no more than a place for rest between walks or during a downpour, I remained in my room which looked over the fine greenery of the park and the lilacs at the entrance, over the green leaves of the tall trees by the lake, sparkling in the sun, and the forest of Meseglise. Yet I looked at all this with pleasure only because I said to myself: "How nice to be able to see so much greenery from my window," until the moment when, in the vast verdant picture, I recognised the steeple of Combray church. Not a representation of the steeple, but the steeple itself which, putting in visible form a distance of miles and years, had come intruding into the midst of the luminous verdure and engraved itself on my windowpane. And if I left my room for a moment, I saw at the end of the corridor, in a little sitting room which faced in another direction, what seemed to be a band of scarlet - for this room was hung with a plain silk, a red one, ready to burst into flames if a ray of sun fell upon it.

The love of Albertine had disappeared. But it seems there exists an involuntary memory, a pale and sterile imitation of the other but longer-lived, just as there are vegetables which are longer lived than man. Once, I woke up in the middle of the night in my room at Tansonville and, still half-asleep, called out: "Albertine!" It was not that I had thought of her or dreamt of her, but a memory in my arm, opening like a flower, had made me fumble behind my back for the bell, as though I had been in my bedroom in Paris. Not finding it, I had called out, thinking that my dead mistress was lying by my side.

During our walks Gilberte intimated to me that Robert was turning away from her, but only in order to run after other women. And it is true that many women encumbered his life, yet always these associations had that quality of purposelessly filling an empty space that often in a house may be seen in objects which are not there to be used. He came several times to Tansonville while I was there and I found him very different from the man I had known. His life had not coarsened him or slowed him down, on the contrary it had given him, although he had resigned his commission on his marriage - the grace and ease of a cavalry officer. This swiftness of movement perhaps symbolised the superficial intrepidity of a man who wants to show that he is not afraid and does not want to give himself time to think. We must mention too, if our account is to be complete, the impatience characteristic of those perpetually bored and cynical men that people inevitably turn into when they are too intelligent for the relatively idle lives they lead, in which their faculties do not have full play.

Becoming - at any rate - much harder in his manner, he now exhibited scarcely any trace of sensibility. Towards Gilberte on the other hand he behaved with an affectation of sentiment carried to the point of theatricality, which was most disagreeable. Not that he was indifferent to her. No, he loved her. But he lied to her all the time and his untruthfulness, if not the actual purpose of his lies, was invariably detected; and then he thought that the only way to extricate himself was to exaggerate to a ridiculous degree the genuine distress he felt at having hurt her. He would arrive at Tansonville obliged, he said, to leave again the next morning because of some business with a certain neighbouring landowner who was supposed to be waiting for him in Paris; but the neighbour, when they happened to meet him near Combray the same evening, would unintentionally expose the lie, of which Robert had neglected to inform him, by saying that he had come to the country for a month's rest. Robert would blush, would observe Gilberte's melancholy and knowing smile, get rid of the blundering friend with a few sharp words, go home before his wife, send her a

desperate note saying that he had told this lie in order
not to hurt her, so that she should not think that he did
not love her (and all this, though Robert thought he was
lying when he wrote it, was in substance true). Like
those hysterics one doesn't have to hypnotise to make
them become such or such a person, he entered
spontaneously and immediately into the character.

Saint-Loup insisted that I should stay on at Tansonville
and once let slip the remark that my coming had been
so great a joy to his wife that it had caused her, as she
had told him, a happiness which lasted a whole evening,
that my unexpected arrival had miraculously saved her
from despair. He asked me to try to persuade her that
he loved her and told me that, though he loved another
woman, he loved her less than his wife and would soon
break with her.

I did not want to borrow Gilberte's copy of *La Fille aux
Yeux d'Or* as she was reading it herself. But she lent me
to read in bed, on that last evening of my stay with her,
a book which produced on me a strong but mixed
impression, which did not, however, prove to be
lasting. It was a newly published volume of the Journal
of the Goncourts. And when I read, my lack of talent for
literature, of which I had had a presentiment long ago
on the Guermantes way and which had been confirmed
during the stay of which this was the last evening - one
of those evenings before a departure when we emerge
from the torpor of habits about to be broken and
attempt to judge ourselves - struck me as something
less to be regretted since literature, if I was to trust the
evidence of this book, had no very profound truths to
reveal.

I stopped, for I was leaving the next morning and it was the hour at which I was habitually summoned by that other master in whose service we spend, every day, a part of our time. The task he assigns we accomplish with our eyes closed. Every morning he hands us back to the master who shares us with him, knowing that, unless he did so, we should be remiss in his own service. Curious, when our intelligence reopens its eyes, to know what we can have done under this master who first makes his slaves lie down and then puts them to work at full speed, the most artful among us try, the moment their task is finished, to take a covert glance. But sleep is racing against them to obliterate the traces of what they would like to see. And after all these centuries we still know very little about the matter.

I closed the Journal of the Goncourts. Prestige of literature! I wished I could have seen the Cottards again, asked them all sorts of details about Elstir, asked permission to visit the Verdurin mansion where I had once dined. But I felt vaguely depressed. Certainly, I had never concealed from myself that I knew neither how to listen nor, once I was not alone, how to look. My eyes were blind to the sort of necklace an old woman might be wearing, and the things I might be told about her pearls never entered my ears. All the same, I had known these people in daily life, I had dined with them often, they were simply the Verdurins and the Duc de Guermantes and the Cottards, and each one of them I had found just as commonplace as my grandmother had. But I decided to ignore the objections against literature raised in my mind by the pages of Goncourt which I had read. Even without taking into account the manifest naivety of this particular diarist, I could in any case reassure myself on various counts. In so far as my own character was concerned, my incapacity for looking and listening, which the Journal had so painfully illustrated to me, was nevertheless not total. There was in me a personage who knew more or less how to look, but it was intermittent, coming to life only in the presence of some general essence common to a number of things, these essences being its nourishment and its joy. Then the personage looked and listened, but at a certain depth only, without my powers of superficial observation being enhanced. The stories people told escaped me, for what interested me was not what they were trying to say but the manner in which they said it and the way in which this manner revealed their character or their foibles; or rather I was interested in what had always, because it gave me specific pleasure, been more the goal of my investigations: the point that was common to one being and another. As soon as I perceived this my intelligence - until that moment slumbering - at once set off joyously in pursuit. The apparent charm of things and people escaped me, because I had not the ability to stop there - I was like a surgeon who beneath the smooth surface of a woman's belly sees the internal disease. If I went to a dinner party I did not see the guests: when I thought I was looking at them, I was in fact examining them.

The result was that all the observations I had succeeded in making during the party took the form of a collection of psychological laws in which the actual remarks of each guest occupied a very small space. But did this take away all merit from my portraits? If one portrait makes certain truths concerning volume, light, movement, does that mean it is inferior to another portrait in which a thousand details omitted in the first are minutely transcribed, a fact which may be of documentary, even historical importance, but is not an artistic truth?

These ideas, tending on the one hand to diminish, and on the other to increase, my regret that I had no gift for literature, were entirely absent from my mind during the long years - in which I had in any case completely renounced the project of writing - which I spent far from Paris receiving treatment in a sanatorium, until there came a time, at the beginning of 1916, when it could no longer get medical staff. I then returned to a Paris very different from the city to which I had come back once before, in August 1914, for a medical consultation.

36

On one of the first evenings of my second return, in 1916, wanting to hear people talk about the only thing that interested me at the time - the war - I went out after dinner to call on Mme Verdurin, who was, with Mme Bontemps, one of the queens of this wartime Paris. Young women now went about all day with tall cylindrical turbans on their heads, and from a sense of patriotic duty wore Egyptian tunics, straight and dark and very "war" over very short skirts; they wore thonged footwear recalling the buskin as worn by Talma, or else long gaiters recalling those of our dear boys at the front; it was, so they said, because they did not forget that it was their duty to these boys at the front that they still decked themselves of an evening not only in flowing dresses but in jewelry which suggested the army. The fashion now was for rings or bracelets made out of fragments of exploded shells or copper bands from 75 millimeter ammunition. And it was also because they never stopped thinking of the dear boys, that when one of their own kin fell they scarcely wore mourning for him, on the pretext "their grief was mingled with pride", which permitted them to replace the cashmere of former days with satin and chiffon, and even to keep their pearls, while observing the tact and propriety of which there is no need to remind Frenchwomen.

The Louvre and all other museums were closed, and when one saw in a newspaper the words "A sensational exhibition" once could be sure the exhibition in question was not one of the paintings but of dresses which aimed at reviving "those refined joys of art of which the women of Paris have for too long been deprived."

So it was that fashion and pleasure had returned.

The dressmakers affirmed that the sadness of the hour - it was true - might prove too strong for feminine energies, were it not that we have so many lofty examples of courage and endurance to contemplate. "So, as we think of our warriors dreaming in their trenches of more comfort and more pretty things for the girl they have left behind them, we shall not pause in our ever more strenuous efforts to create dresses that answer the needs of the moment."

As for charity, the thought of all the miseries that had sprung from the invasion, of all the wounded and disabled, meant naturally that it was obliged to develop forms "more ingenious than ever before," and this meant that the ladies in tall turbans were obliged to spend the latter part of the afternoon at "teas" round a bridge table, discussing the news from the front, while their cars waited at the door with a handsome soldier in the driver's seat who chatted to the footman.

It was, moreover, not only the headdresses above the ladies' faces that were new, the faces were new themselves. The lady who had known the Guermantes since 1914 looked upon the lady who had been introduced in 1916 as an upstart, greeted her with the air of a dowager, and admitted with a little grimace that no one even knew for certain whether or not she was married. "It is all rather nauseating" concluded the lady of 1914, who would have liked the cycle of new admission to have come to a halt after herself. The Saint Euverte salon was a faded banner now, and the presence beneath it of the greatest artists would have attracted nobody. But people would run to listen to the secretary of one of these same artists holding forth in the houses of the new turbaned ladies whose winged and chattering invasion filled Paris. The ladies of the first Directory had a queen who was young and beautiful and was called Mme Tallien. Those of the second had two who were old and ugly and were called Mme Verdurin and Mme Bontemps. Who could now hold it against Mme Bontemps that in the Dreyfus Affair her husband had played a role? In society (and this phenomenon is merely a particular case of a much more general law) novelties excite horror only so long as they have not been assimilated and enveloped by reassuring elements. It was the same with Dreyfusism as with the marriage between Saint-Loup and the daughter of Odette which had at first produced such an outcry. Now that "everybody" was seen at the parties given by the Saint-Loups, Gilberte might have had the morals of Odette herself but people would have gone there just the same.   Dreyfusism was now integrated in a scheme of respectable and familiar things. As for whether intrinsically it was good or bad, the idea no more entered anybody's head. It was no longer *shocking* and that was all that mattered.

Be that as it may, they came, in search of exactly the same thing as in the old days, that is to say a social pleasure that satisfied their need to discuss with others like themselves the incidents about which they had read in the newspapers. Mme Verdurin said "Come at 5 o'clock to talk about the war" as she would have said in the past: "Come and talk about the Affair".

Now that Mme Verdurin could get anyone she wanted to come to her house, people were surprised to see her make advances to Odette, the general opinion being that Odette could add nothing to the brilliant set the little group had become. But a prolonged separation in some cases reawakens feelings of friendship. "I can't think why we no longer see her here" she said. "She may have fallen out with me, I haven't with her. After all, what harm have I done her? It was in my house she met her husbands. If she wants to come back, let her know the door is open." These words were passed on, but without success. Mme Verdurin waited in vain for Odette, until events which will come to our notice later brought about, for entirely different reasons, what intercession had been unable to achieve. So rarely do we meet either with easy success or with irreversible defeat.

37

Before the hour at which the afternoon tea-parties
came to an end, in the still light sky one saw, far off,
little brown dots one might have taken, in the blue
evening, for midges or birds. In the same way, when we
see a mountain at a great distance one can imagine it to
be a cloud. But because one knows this cloud is huge,
solid and resistant one's emotions are stirred. And I too
was moved by the thought the brown dot was neither
midge nor bird but an aeroplane keeping guard over
Paris. When the time came for dinner the restaurants
were full; and if, passing in the street, I saw a wretched
soldier on leave, escaped for six days from the constant
death and about to return, halt his gaze for a moment
upon the illuminated windows, I suffered as I had in the
hotel at Balbec when fishermen used to watch us at
dinner, but more now because I knew the misery of the
soldier is greater than that of the poor since it combines
in itself all miseries. It was with a philosophical shake of
the head, without hatred, that on the eve of setting out
again for the war the soldier would say to himself, as he
saw the shirkers jostling one another in their efforts to
secure a table: "You'd never know there was a war on
here." Then at half past nine, before anyone had time
to finish dinner, the lights were all suddenly turned out
so that at nine thirty five the second jostling of shirkers

snatching their overcoats took place in a mysterious half-darkness which might have been that of a room in which slides are being shown on a magic lantern.

But at any later hour for those who, like myself on the evening I am going to describe, had dinner at home and were going out to see friends, Paris was blacker than the Combray of my childhood; the visits people paid one another were like the visits of country neighbours. If Albertine had been alive, how delightful it would have been to arrange to meet her under the arcades! At first I would have seen nothing, thinking she had failed to turn up, when suddenly I should have seen one of her grey dresses emerge from the black wall, then her smiling eyes which had already seen me, and we could have walked along with our arms round each other without any fear of being disturbed and then gone home. But alas I was alone and felt as if I was setting out to pay a visit in the country, like those Swann used to pay us after dinner, without meeting more people along the little tow-path than I now met in the streets, transformed into winding rustic lanes, between Sainte-Clotilde and the Rue Bonaparte. Or again - since the effect of those fragments of landscape which travel in obedience to the moods of the weather was no longer nullified by surroundings which had become invisible - on evenings when the wind was chasing an icy shower of rain I had - now much more strongly - the impression of being on the shore of that raging sea of which I had once so longingly dreamed than I had had when I was actually at Balbec. And other natural features also, which had not existed in Paris hitherto, helped to create the illusion one had just got out of the train and arrived in the depth of the country;

for example the light and shadow on the ground on evenings when the moon was shining. There were effects of moonlight normally unknown in towns, when the rays of the moon lay upon the snow on the Boulevard Haussmann, untouched by the broom of any sweeper, as they would have lain upon a glacier in the Alps. Against this snow the silhouettes of trees were outlined clear and pure, with the delicacy they have in Japanese paintings or certain backgrounds of Raphael; and on the ground at the foot of the tree its shadow as often one sees trees' shadows in the country, when the light polishes some meadow in which they are planted at intervals. In the squares the public fountains looked like statues by a sculptor who had decided to marry bronze to crystal. On these exceptional days all the houses were black. But in the Spring here and there, defying the regulations, a private house, or one floor of a house, or simply one room of one floor had failed to close its shutters and appeared, mysteriously supported by dark shadows, to be no more than a projection of light, an apparition without substance.

Then one passed on and nothing more interrupted the rustic tramp, wholesome and monotonous, of one's feet through the darkness.

It was a long time since I had seen any of the personages who have been mentioned in this work. In 1914, during two months I had spent in Paris, I caught a glimpse of M de Charlus and seen something of Saint-Loup, the latter only twice. The second occasion was certainly that on which he had been most himself; he had quite effaced that disagreeable impression he made

on me at Tansonville, and I once more recognised in
him all the fine qualities of his earlier days.

"Are we in for a long war?" I said to Saint-Loup. "No, I
believe it will be very short," he replied. But here, as
always, his arguments were bookish. "Bearing in mind
the prophecies of Moltke," he said to me, as if I had
read it, "the decree of the 28th October about the
command of large formation; you will see that the
replacement of peacetime reserves has not been
organised or even foreseen, a thing which authorities
could not have failed to do if the war were likely to be a
long one." It seemed to me that the decree could be
interpreted not as proof that the war would be short,
but as a failure to foresee that it would be long, the
truth being they suspected neither the appalling
wastage of material of every kind that would take place
in a war of stable fronts nor the interdependence of
different theatres of operations.

I had, in any case, not remained long in Paris but had
returned very soon to my sanatorium. Although in
principle the doctor's treatment consisted in isolation, I
had been allowed to receive a letter from Gilberte and a
letter from Robert. Gilberte wrote (this was in about
September 1914) that, however much she would have
liked to stay in Paris in order to get news of Robert
more easily, the constant raids on the city had caused
her such alarm for her little girl that she had fled by the
last train to leave for Combray, that the train had not
even got as far as Combray, and that it was only thanks
to a peasant's cart on which she had a journey of ten
hours, that she had succeeded in reaching
Tansonville! "And there, imagine what awaited your old

friend," she concluded her letter. "I had left Paris to escape from the German aeroplanes, supposing that at Tansonville I should be perfectly safe. Before I had been there two days you will never imagine what turned up: Germans, who, having defeated our troops near La Fere, were overrunning the district. A German staff, with a regiment just behind it, presented itself at the gates of Tansonville and I was obliged to take them in, and not a hope of getting away - no more trains - nothing." Whether the German staff had really behaved well, or whether it was right to detect in Gilberte's letter the influence, by contagion, of the spirit of those Guermantes who were of Bavarian stock and related to the highest aristocracy of Germany, she was lavish in her praise of the perfect breeding of the staff officers, and even of the soldiers who had only asked her for "permission to pick a few of the forget-me-nots growing near the pond", which she contrasted with the disorderly violence of the fleeing French.

In any case, if Gilberte's letter was in some ways impregnated with the spirit of the Guermantes, the letter I received several months later from Robert was much more Saint-Loup, and reflected the liberal culture which he had acquired. Altogether it was a delightful letter. Unfortunately, he did not talk about strategy as he had in our conversations at Doncieres, nor did he tell me to what extent he considered that the war confirmed or invalidated the principles which he had then expounded to me.

All he said was that since 1914 there had in reality been a series of wars, the lessons of each one influencing the conduct of the one that followed. For example, the theory of the "break through" had been supplemented by a new idea: that it was necessary, before breaking through, for the ground held by the enemy to be completely devastated by artillery. But then it had been found that on the contrary this devastation made it impossible for the infantry and artillery to advance over ground in which thousands of shell-holes created as many obstacles. "War" he wrote, "does not escape the laws of our old friend Hegel. It is in a state of perpetual becoming."

And now, on my second return to Paris, I had received, the day after I arrived, another letter from Gilberte, who had doubtless forgotten the letter I have described , for in this new letter her departure from Paris at the end of 1914 was presented in a very different light. "Perhaps you do not know, my dear friend," she wrote "that I have now been at Tansonville for nearly two years. I arrived here at the same time as the Germans. Everybody had tried to prevent me from leaving. I was regarded as mad. 'What,' my friends said, 'here you are safe in Paris and you want to go off to enemy occupied territory just when everybody is trying to escape from it.' But I can't help it; if I have one good quality it is that I am not a coward, or perhaps I should say, I am loyal, and when I knew that my beloved Tansonville was threatened, I simply could not leave our old bailiff to defend it alone. I felt my place was by his side. And it was, in fact, thanks to this decision that I succeeded in more or less saving the house when all the other big houses in the neighbourhood, abandoned by their panic-stricken owners, were almost without exception reduced to ruins - and in saving not only the house but the collections too, which dear Papa was so fond of." Gilberte was now persuaded she had gone to Tansonville not, as she had written to me in 1914, in order to escape the Germans but on the contrary in order to face them. They had, as a matter of fact, not stayed long at Tansonville, but since then the house had witnessed a constant coming and going of soldiers, far more intensive than that marching up and down the streets of Combray which had once drawn tears to the eyes of Francoise, and Gilberte had not ceased, as she said, this time quite truly, to live the life of the front. The newspapers spoke of her conduct and there was some question of giving her a decoration. The end of the letter was absolutely truthful. "You have no idea what this war is like, my dear friend, or of the importance that a road, a bridge, a height can assume. How often have I thought of you, of those walks of ours together which you made so delightful, through all this now ravaged countryside, where vast battles are fought to gain possession of some path, some slope which you once loved and which we explored together! Probably, like me, you did not imagine that obscure Roussainville and boring Meseglise, where our letters used to be brought from and where the doctor was once fetched when you were ill, would ever be famous places. Well, my dear friend, they have become for ever a part of history, with the same claim to glory as Austerlitz or Valmy. The battle of Meseglise lasted for more than eight months; the Germans lost in it more than six hundred thousand men, they destroyed Meseglise but they did not capture it. As for the shortcut up the hill which you were so fond of and which we used to call the hawthorn path, where you claim that as a small child you fell in love with me (whereas I assure you in all truthfulness it was I who was in love with you), I cannot tell you how important it has become. The huge field of corn upon which it emerges is the famous Hill 307 which you must have seen in the bulletins. The French blew up the little bridge over the Vivonne which you said did not remind you of your childhood as much as you would have wished, and the Germans have thrown other bridges across the river. For a year and a half they held one half of Combray and the French the other."

The day after I received this letter, that is to say two days before the evening on which, as I have described, I made my way through the dark streets with the sound of my footsteps in my ears and all these memories revolving in my mind, Saint-Loup - arrived from the front and very shortly to return to it - had come to see me for a few moments, and the mere announcement of his visit had violently moved me.

When Saint-Loup came into my room I had gone up to him with that feeling of shyness, that impression of something supernatural which was in fact induced by all soldiers on leave and which one feels when one enters the presence of a man suffering from a fatal disease, who still nevertheless goes for walks. It seemed (for upon those who had not lived, as I had, at a distance from Paris, there had descended Habit, which cuts off from things we have witnessed a number of times the root of profound impression and of thought which gives them their real meaning) almost that there was something cruel in these leaves granted to the men at the front. When they first came on leave, one said to oneself: "They will refuse to go back." And indeed they came not merely from places which seemed to us unreal, because we had only heard them spoken of in the newspapers; it was from the shores of death, whither they would soon return, that they came to spend a few moments in our midst, incomprehensible to us, filling us with tenderness and terror and a feeling of mystery, like phantoms we summon whom we dare not question, and who could, in any case, only reply: "You cannot possibly imagine."

For it is extraordinary how, in the survivors of battle, or in living men hypnotised or dead men summoned by a medium, the only effect of contact with mystery is to increase the significance of the things people say. Such were my feelings when I greeted Robert, who still had a scar on his forehead, more august and more mysterious in my eyes than the imprint left upon the earth by a giant's foot. And I had not dared to put a question to him and he had made only the simplest remarks that even differed very little from the ones he might have made before the war, as though people, in spite of the war, continued to be what they were. The tone of conversation was the same, only the subject matter differed - and even that not very much!

I had gone on walking as I turned over in my mind this recent meeting with Saint-Loup and had come a long way out of my way; I was almost at the Pont des Invalides. The night was as beautiful as in 1914, and the threat to Paris was as great. In an instant the streets became totally black. At moments only, an enemy aeroplane flying very low lit up the spot upon which it wished to drop a bomb. I set off, but very soon I was lost. I thought of when, on my way to La Raspeliere, I had met an aeroplane and my horse had reared as at the apparition of a god. Now, I thought, it would be a different meeting - with the god of evil, who would kill me. I started to walk faster in order to escape, like a traveller pursued by a tidal wave; I groped my way round dark squares from which I could find no way out. At last the flames of a blazing building showed me where I was and I got back on to the right road, while all the time the shells burst noisily above my head.

38

 My departure from Paris was delayed by a piece of
news which caused me such grief that I was for some
time rendered incapable of traveling.   This was the
death of Robert de Saint-Loup, killed two days after his
return to the front while covering the retreat of his
men.

Never had any man felt less hatred for a nation than he;
the last words I heard on his lips, six days before he
died, were the opening words of a Schumann song he
had started to hum in German on my staircase, until I
made him desist because of the neighbours. For several
days I remained shut up in my room, thinking of him. I
recalled his arrival the first time at Balbec when, in an
almost white suit, with eyes greenish and mobile like
the waves, he had crossed the hall whose windows gave
on to the sea. I recalled the very special being he had

seemed to be, for whose friendship I had so greatly wished. That wish had been realised beyond what I should have thought possible. Later I had come to understand the many great virtues and something else as well which lay concealed behind his elegant appearance. All this he had given without counting the cost, every day, as much on the last day when he advanced to attack a trench because it was his habit to place at the service of others all that he possessed. The fact I had seen him really so little but in circumstances so diverse and separated by so many intervals - in that hall at Balbec, the cafe at Rivebelle, the cavalry barracks and military dinners in Doncieres, at the theatre, the house of the Princesse de Guermantes - had the effect of giving his life pictures more striking and more sharply defined and his death a grief more lucid than in the case of people whom we have loved more, but with whom our association has been so continuous that the image we retain of them is a sort of vague average.

39

The new sanatorium to which I withdrew was no more successful curing me than the first, and many years passed. During the train journey which eventually took me back to Paris, my lack of talent for literature - a defect I had first discovered long ago on the Guermantes way which I had again recognised and been still more saddened by, in the course of the daily walks with Gilberte before returning to dine late at Tansonville, and which on the eve of my departure from that house I had come very near to identifying, after reading some pages of the Goncourt Journal, with the vanity of literature - this thought, less painful perhaps but more melancholy still if I referred it not to a private infirmity of my own but to the nonexistence of the ideal in which I had believed - this thought which for a long time had not entered my mind struck me afresh and

with a force more painful than ever before. The train
had stopped, I remember, in open country. The sun
was shining on a row of trees that followed the railway,
flooding the upper halves with light. "Trees," I thought,
"you no longer have anything to say to me. My heart
has grown cold and no longer hears you. I am in the
midst of nature. Well, it is with indifference. If I ever
thought of myself as a poet, I know now that I am
not. Perhaps in the new part of my life which is about
to begin, human beings may yet inspire in me what
nature can no longer say. But the years in which I might
have been able to sing *her* praise will never return."   I
knew that I knew myself to be worthless.

If I really had the soul of an artist, surely I would be
feeling pleasure at the sight of this curtain of trees lit by
the setting sun, these little flowers on the bank which
lifted themselves almost to the steps of my
compartment, flowers whose petals I was able to count
but whose colour I would not attempt to describe, for
can one hope to transmit to the reader a pleasure one
has not felt? A little later I noticed with the same
absence of emotion the glitter of gold and orange which
the sun splashed upon the windows of a house; and
finally, as the evening advanced, I had seen another
house which appeared to be built out of a strange pink
substance. But I had made these observations with the
same indifference as if, walking in a garden with a lady, I
had seen a pane of glass and, a little further on, an
object of alabaster-like material, the unusual colour of
which had failed to draw me out of boredom, but out of
politeness toward the lady, in order to show that I had
noticed these colours, I had pointed in passing to the
tinted glass and the fragment of stucco. In the same

way, to satisfy my conscience, I indicated to myself now the flame-like reflections in the windows and the pink transparency of the house. But the companion whose attention I had drawn to these curious effects had taken cognisance of the colours without any joy.

My long absence from Paris had not prevented old friends from continuing faithfully to send me invitations, and when on my return I found - together with one to a tea-party given by Berma for her daughter and son-in-law - another to an afternoon party with music at the house of the Prince de Guermantes, the gloomy reflections which had passed through my mind in the train were not the least of the motives which urged me to accept. Really, I said to myself, what point is there in forgoing the pleasures of social life if, as seems to be the case, the "work" which for so long I have been hoping to start, is something I am not made for.

When I thought of what Bergotte had said to me: "You are ill, but one cannot pity you for you have the joys of the mind" how mistaken he had been about me! How little joy there was in this sterile lucidity! Even if sometimes perhaps I had pleasures I sacrificed them always to one woman or another; so that had fate granted me another hundred years of life and sound health as well, it would merely have added a series of extensions to an already tedious existence, which there seemed to be no point in prolonging.

But it is sometimes at the moment when we think everything is lost that the intimation arrives which may save us; one has knocked at all the doors which lead nowhere, and then the only door which one can enter opens of its own accord. Revolving the gloomy thoughts I just recorded, I had entered the courtyard of the Guermantes mansion and in my absent-minded state had failed to see a car coming towards me; the chauffeur gave a shout and I just had time to step out of the way, but as I moved I tripped against the uneven paving-stones. When, recovering my balance, I put my foot on a stone which was slightly lower than its neighbour, all of my discouragement vanished and in its place was that same happiness which at various epochs of my life had been given to me by the sight of trees which I had thought I recognized near Balbec, by the sight of the twin steeples of Martinville, by the flavour of a madeleine dipped in tea, and by all those other sensations of which I have spoken and which the last works of Vinteuil had seemed to combine. Just as, at the moment when I tasted the madeleine, all anxiety about the future had disappeared, so now those that a few seconds ago had assailed me on the subject of my literary gifts were removed as if by magic.

I had followed no new train of reasoning, discovered no decisive argument, but the difficulties which had seemed insoluble a moment ago had lost all importance. The happiness I felt was unquestionably the same as that which I had felt when I tasted the madeleine soaked in tea. But if on that occasion I had put off the task of searching for the profounder causes of my emotion, this time I was determined not to resign myself to a failure to understand them. In my desire to seize them - as afraid to move as I had been on the occasion when I had continued to savour the taste of the madeleine while I tried to draw into my consciousness whatever it recalled to me - I continued, ignoring the amusement of the chauffeurs, to stagger with one foot on the higher paving stone and the other on the lower. Every time I succeeded, forgetting the party, in recapturing what I had felt when I first placed my feet on the ground this way, again the dazzling and indistinct vision fluttered near me, as if to say: "Seize me as I pass if you can, and try to solve the riddle of happiness." And almost at once I recognised the vision: it was Venice, of which my memory had never told me anything, but which the sensation I had once experienced as I stood upon two uneven stones in the baptistery of St Mark's had, recurring a moment ago, restored to me complete with all the other sensations linked on that day to that particular sensation, all of which had been waiting in their place in the series of forgotten days. In the same way the taste of the little madeleine had recalled Combray to me. But why had the images of Combray and of Venice, at these two different moments, given me a joy which was like a certainty and which sufficed, without any other proof, to make death a matter of indifference to me?

Still asking myself this question, and determined to find the answer, I entered the Guermantes mansion, because always we give precedence over the inner task that we have to perform to the outward role which we are playing which was, for me at this moment, that of guest. But when I had gone upstairs, a butler requested me to wait for a few minutes in a little sitting room used as a library until the end of the piece of music being played. A servant chanced to knock a spoon against a plate and again that same happiness which had come to me from the uneven paving-stones poured into me and I recognised that what seemed to me now so delightful was that same row of trees I had found tedious to observe and describe but which I had just now for a moment, in a sort of daze - supposed to be before my eyes, so forcibly had the noise of the spoon knocking against the plate given me, until I had time to remember where I was, the illusion of the noise of the hammer with which a railwayman had done something to a wheel of the train while we stopped near the little wood. And then it seemed as though the signs which were to bring me, on this day of all days, out of my disheartened state and restore to me my faith in literature, were thronging eagerly about me, for a butler who had long been in the service of the Prince having recognised me and brought to me in the library a selection of petits fours and a glass of orangeade, I wiped my mouth with the napkin which he had given me and instantly, as though I had been the character in the Arabian Nights who unwittingly accomplishes the very rite which can cause to appear, visible to him alone, a docile genie ready to convey him a great distance, a new vision passed before my eyes. I thought that the servant had just opened the window on to the beach and that all things invited me to go down and stroll along the promenade while the tide was high, for the napkin had precisely the same degree of stiffness and starch as the towel with which I had found it so awkward to dry my face in front of the window on the first day of my arrival at Balbec, and this napkin now, in the library of the Prince de Guermantes' house, unfolded for me - concealed within its smooth surfaces and folds - an ocean green and blue like the tail of a peacock. And what I found myself enjoying was not merely these colours but a whole instant of my life on whose summit they rested, an instant which had been no doubt an aspiration towards them and which some feeling of fatigue or sadness had perhaps prevented me from enjoying at Balbec but which now, freed from what is necessarily imperfect in external perception, pure and disembodied, caused me to swell with happiness.

The piece of music might end at any moment and I might be obliged to enter the drawing room. So I forced myself to try as quickly as possible to discern the essence I had just experienced three times within a few minutes, and to extract the lesson they might yield. The thought there is a vast difference between the real impression we have of a thing and the artificial impression of it we form for ourselves when we attempt by an act of will to imagine it did not long detain me. Remembering with what indifference Swann had been able to speak of the days when he had been loved, and on the other hand the sudden pain he had been caused by the little phrase of Vinteuil when it gave him back the days themselves (just as they were when he had felt them in the past) I understood clearly that what the sensation of the uneven paving-stones, the stiffness of the napkin, the taste of the madeleine had reawakened in me had no connection with what I frequently tried to recall to myself of Venice, Balbec, Combray, with the help of memory; and I understood that the reason life may be judged trivial although at certain moments it seems to us so beautiful is that we form our judgments, ordinarily, on the evidence not of life itself but of those images which preserve nothing of life. I noticed that our real impressions derive from the following; the slightest word we have said, the most insignificant action we have performed was surrounded by, and colored by the reflection of, things which logically had no connection with it. Things, however, in the midst of which - here the pink reflection of the evening upon the flower covered wall of a country restaurant, a feeling of hunger, the desire for women, the pleasure of luxury, there the blue volutes of the morning sea and, enveloped in them, phrases of music half emerging like the shoulders of water-nymphs - the simplest act or gesture remains immured as within a thousand sealed vessels, each one of them different one from another, vessels disposed over the whole range of our years, during which we have never ceased to change. It is true we have accomplished these changes imperceptibly; but between the memory which brusquely returns to us and our present state, the distance is such that it alone would make it impossible to compare one with the other. Yes: if, owing to the work of oblivion, the returning memory can throw no bridge, form no connecting link between itself and the present, if it remains in the context of its own place and date, if it keeps its distance, its isolation in the hollow of a valley or upon the highest peak of a mountain summit, for this very reason it causes us suddenly to breathe a new air, an air which is new precisely because we have breathed it in the past, that purer air which the poets have vainly tried to situate in paradise and which could induce so profound a renewal only if it had been breathed before, since the true paradises are the paradises we have lost.

And I observed in passing that for the work of art which I now felt myself ready to undertake, this distinctness of events would entail considerable difficulties. For I should have to execute the parts of my work in a succession of different materials; what would be suitable for mornings beside the sea would be quite wrong if I wanted to depict evenings at Rivebelle when the heat began to resolve into fragments and the last water-colours of the day were still visible in the sky.

Over all these thoughts I skimmed rapidly, for another inquiry demanded my attention. The inquiry, which on previous occasions I had postponed, into the cause of this felicity which I had just experienced, into the certitude with which it imposed itself. And this cause I began to divine as I compared these diverse happy impressions, diverse yet with this in common; that I experienced them at the present moment and at the same time in the context of a distant moment, so that the past was made to encroach upon the present and I was made to doubt whether I was in one or the other.

The truth was that these impressions were outside time.

This explained why my anxiety on the subject of my death had ceased when I had recognized the taste of the madeleine. This had only manifested itself on those rare occasions when the miracle of an analogy had made me escape from the present. And only this had the power to perform that task which had always defeated the efforts of my memory and intellect, the power to rediscover the Time That Was Lost.

And perhaps, if just now I had been disposed to think Bergotte wrong when he spoke of the life of the mind and its joys, it was because what I thought of at that moment as "the life of the mind" was logical reasoning which had no connection with what existed in me at this moment - an error like the one which had made me find society and life tedious because I judged them on the evidence of untrue recollections, whereas now, now that three times in succession there had been reborn within me a veritable moment of the past, my appetite for life was immense.

A moment of the past? Perhaps very much more: something common both to the past and the present, much more than either of them. So often reality had disappointed me because at the instant my senses perceived it my imagination could not apply itself to it, in that we can only imagine what is absent. Now, suddenly, this law had been neutralized by a sensation - the noise made both by the spoon and the hammer for instance - so my imagination was permitted to savour it and what normally it never apprehends: a fragment of time in the pure state. The being which had been reborn in me with a shudder of happiness, this being is nourished only by the essences of things, in these alone does it find its delight. In the observation of the present, where the senses cannot feed it, it languishes, as it does in the consideration of a past made arid by the intellect. But let a noise or a scent be heard or smelt again in the present and at the same time in the past, immediately the essence of things is liberated and our true self which seemed - perhaps for long years - to be dead, is awakened. A minute freed from the order of time has created in us the man freed from the order of time.

This man should have confidence in his joy. Even if the simple taste of a madeleine does not seem to contain within it the reasons, one can understand that the word "death" should have no meaning for him; situated outside time, why should he fear the future? So complete are these resurrections of the past during the second that they last, they force our whole self to believe it is surrounded by these places or at least to waver between them and the places we are, in a dazed uncertainty such as we feel sometimes when an indescribably beautiful vision presents itself at the moment of our falling asleep.

Fragments of existence withdrawn from Time: these then were perhaps what the being three times, four times brought back to life within me had just tasted. I was vaguely aware the pleasure this had, at rare intervals, given me was the only genuine pleasure I had known.

After I had dwelt for some time upon these resurrections, the thought came to me that certain impressions had solicited my attention in a fashion somewhat similar, except they concealed within them not a sensation dating from an earlier time, but a truth, a precious image I sought to uncover. The ideas formed by the pure intelligence have no more than a logical, possible truth. The book whose hieroglyphs are not traced by us is the only book that really belongs to us. What we have not had to decipher, to elucidate with our own efforts, what was clear before we looked at it is not ours. From ourselves comes only that which we drag forth from the obscurity which lies within. I had arrived at the conclusion that in fashioning a work of art we are by no means free, that we do not choose how we shall make it but that it pre-exists us and therefore we are obliged to discover it. But this discovery which art obliges us to make, is it not, I thought, really the discovery of our true life, which differs so greatly from what we think it is that when a chance happening brings us an authentic memory of it we are filled with an immense happiness?

Nor is this all. A thing which we saw, a book which we read at a certain period does not merely remain forever conjoined to what existed then around us; it remains also united to what we ourselves then were. If, even in thought, I pick from the bookshelf *Francois le Champi*, immediately there rises within me a child who takes my place, and who reads it as he read it once before, with the same impression of what the weather was like then in the garden, the same dreams that were then shaping themselves in his mind, the same anguish about the next day. Or if I see something from another period, it is a young man who comes to life. So that my personality of today may be compared to an abandoned quarry, which supposes everything it contains to be uniform and monotonous, but from which memory, selecting here and there, can extract statues. An hour is not merely an hour, it is a vase of scents and sounds and projects and climates, and what we call reality is a certain connection between these sensations and the memories which envelop us - a unique connection which the writer has to rediscover in order to link for ever in his phrase the two sets of phenomena which reality joins together. Truth - and life too - can be attained by us only when, by comparing a quality common to two sensations, we succeed in extracting their common essence and in reuniting them to each other, liberated from the contingencies of time.

But art, if it means awareness of our own life, means also awareness of the lives of other people - for style for the writer, no less than colour for the painter, is a question not of technique but of vision; it is the revelation of the qualitative difference which, if there were no art, would remain for ever the secret of every individual. Through art alone we are able to emerge from ourselves, to know what another person sees. This work of the artist, this struggle to discern something that is different from them, is the reverse of those everyday lives we live with our gaze averted by vanity and passion and intellect, and habit too, when they smother our true impressions beneath a whole heap of verbal concepts and practical goals we falsely call life. As for the truths which the intellectual faculty - even that of the greatest minds - gathers in the open, their value may be very great, but they are like drawings with a hard outline and no perspective; they have no depth because no depths have had to be traversed in order to reach them, because they have not been re-created.

40

At this moment the butler came in to tell me the first piece of music was finished so I could leave the library and go into the rooms where the party was taking place. And thereupon I remembered where I was. For a few seconds I did not understand why it was I had difficulty recognising the master of the house and the guests and why everyone appeared to have put on a disguise - in most cases a powdered wig - which changed him completely. The Prince himself, as he stood receiving his guests, still had that genial look of a king in a fairy story which I had remarked in him the first time I had been to his house, but today, he had got himself up in a white beard and dragged his feet. Whereas at a dress ball civility leads one to exaggerate the difficulty of recognising the person beneath the disguise, here an instinct warned me to do the contrary; I felt the success of the disguise was no longer flattering because the transformation was not intentional. And I realised something: that every party, grand or simple, which takes place after a long interval, provided it brings together some of the people whom one knew in the past, gives one the impression of a masquerade, at which one is most genuinely "intrigued" by the identity of the guests, but with the novel feature that the disguises cannot, when the party is over, be wiped off.

This study in caricature was rather a puppet-show which was both scientific and philosophical. A puppet-show, yes, but one in which, in order to identify the puppets with the people one had known in the past, it was necessary to read on several planes at once, planes that lay behind the visible aspect of the puppets and gave them depth and forced one to study them at the same time with one's eyes and with one's memory. These were puppets bathed in the immaterial colours of the years, puppets which exteriorised Time, Time which is invisible and to become visible seeks bodies, which it seizes to display its magic lantern upon.

In some of the guests at the party the successive replacement, accomplished in my absence, of each cell by other cells, had brought about a change so complete, a metamorphosis so entire that I could have dined opposite them in a restaurant without suspecting I had known them in the past.   And now I began to understand what old age was - old age, which perhaps of all the realities is the one of which we preserve for longest in our life a purely abstract conception, looking at calendars, dating our letters, seeing our friends marry and then in turn the children of our friends, and yet not understanding what all this means until the day when a grandson of a woman we once knew, whom instinctively we treat as a contemporary, smiles as though we were making fun of him - and I began to understand too what death meant and love and the joys of the spiritual life, the usefulness of suffering, a vocation. For if names had lost most of their individuality for me, words on the other hand now began to reveal their full significance. The beauty of images is situated in front of things, that of ideas behind them. So that the first sort of beauty ceases to astonish us as soon as we have reached the things themselves, but the second is something we understand only when we have passed beyond them.

In some of the guests I recognised after a while not merely themselves but themselves as they had been in the past. And yet, in contrast with these, I had the surprise of talking to men and women whom I remembered as unendurable and who had now lost almost every one of their defects, possibly because life, by disappointing or by gratifying their desires, had rid them of most of their conceit or their bitterness. The essential marks of old age were manifested in them, but old age here was a moral phenomenon. Nobody was exempt from change.

 It would be impossible to depict our relationship with anyone whom we have even slightly known without passing in review the different settings of our life. Each individual - and I was myself one of these individuals - was a measure of duration for me, in virtue of the revolutions which like some heavenly body he had accomplished not only on his own axis but also around myself. And surely the awareness of all these different planes within which Time seemed to dispose the different elements of my life had added a new beauty to those resurrections of the past which my memory had effected while I was following my thoughts alone in the library, since memory by itself, when it introduces the past into the present - just as it was at the moment when it was itself the present - suppresses the mighty dimension of Time which is the dimension in which life is lived.

Thus was the task before me, a task which would not end until I had achieved what I had so ardently desired in my walks on the Guermantes way and thought to be impossible, just as I had thought it impossible, as I came home at the end of those walks, that I should ever get used to going to bed without kissing my mother or, later, to the idea that Albertine loved women. In the end, neither our greatest fears nor our greatest hopes are beyond the limits of our strength.

Yes, it was time to set to work. It was high time. But - and this anxiety had gripped me as soon as I entered the drawing-room, was there still time and was I still in a fit condition to undertake the task? For one thing, a necessary condition of my work was a study of impressions which had first to be recreated through the memory, but my memory was old and tired. The mind has landscapes which it is allowed to contemplate only for a certain space of time. In my life I had been like a painter climbing a road high above a lake, a view of which is denied to him by a curtain of rocks and trees. Suddenly through a gap he sees the lake, its expanse is before him, he takes up his brushes. But already the night is at hand, which no dawn will follow. How could I not be anxious, seeing that nothing was yet begun and though I could still hope that I had some years to live, my hour might on the other hand strike almost at once? For the fundamental fact was that I had a body, and this meant I was perpetually threatened by a double danger, internal and external, though to speak thus was merely a convenience, the truth being that the internal danger is also external, since it is the body that it threatens. Indeed it is the possession of a body that is the great danger to the mind.

In my awareness of the approach of death I resembled a dying soldier, and like him too, before I died, I had something to write. But my task was longer than his, my words had to reach more than a single person. My task was long. By day, the most I could hope for was to sleep. If I worked, it would be at night. But I should need many nights, a hundred perhaps, or even a thousand. And I should live in the anxiety of not knowing whether the master of my destiny might not prove less indulgent than the Sultan Shahriyar, whether in the morning he would consent to a further reprieve and permit me to resume my narrative the following evening.

Ah! If only I now possessed the strength which had still been intact on that evening brought back to my mind by the sight of *Francois le Champi*! Was not that the evening when my mother had abdicated her authority, the evening from which dated, together with the slow death of my grandmother, the decline of my health and my will? All these things had been decided in that moment when, no longer able to bear the prospect of waiting till morning to place my lips upon my mother's face, I had jumped out of bed and gone in my night-shirt to post myself at the window through which the moonlight entered my room until I should hear the sounds of M. Swann's departure. My parents had gone with him to the door, I had heard the garden gate open, give a peal of its bell, and close...

When the bell of the garden gate had pealed, I already existed and from that moment onwards, for me still to be able to hear that peal, there must have been no break, no single second at which I had ceased existing, from being myself, since that moment from long ago still adhered to me and I could still find it again, could retrace my steps to it, merely by descending within myself.

In this vast dimension which I had not known myself to possess, the date on which I had heard the noise of the garden bell at Combray - that far distant noise which nevertheless was within me -was a point from which I might start to make measurements. And I felt, as I say, a sensation of weariness and almost of terror at the thought that all this length of Time had not only, without interruption, been lived by me, that it was my life, was in fact me, but also that I was compelled so long as i was alive to keep it attached to me, that it supported me and that, perched on its giddy summit, I could not myself make a movement without displacing it. A feeling of vertigo seized me as I looked down beneath me, yet within me, as though from a height, which was my own height, of many leagues, at the long series of the years.

I understood now why it was the Duc de Guermantes, who to my surprise, when I had seen him sitting on a chair, had seemed to me so little aged although he had so many more years beneath him than I had, had presently, when he rose to his feet and tried to stand upon them, advanced with difficulty, trembling like a leaf, upon the summit of his eighty three years, as though men spend their lives perched upon living stilts which never cease to grow, making it in the end both difficult and perilous for them to walk and raising them to an eminence from which they suddenly fall. And I was terrified by the thought that the stilts beneath my own feet might already have reached that height; it seemed to me that quite soon now I might be too weak to maintain my hold upon a past which already went down so far. So, if I were given long enough to accomplish my work, I should not fail, even if the effect were to make them resemble monsters, to describe men as occupying so considerable a place, compared with the restricted place which is reserved for them in space, a place on the contrary prolonged past measure, for simultaneously, like giants plunged into the years, they touch the distant epochs through which they have lived, between which so many days have come to range themselves - in Time.

ABOUT THE AUTHOR

Marcel Proust wrote and published *a la Recherche du Temps Perdu* in the early 1900s, around the period of the first World War.   The original version is approximately 4,200 pages long.   It's title has been translated in various ways, including 'In Search of Lost Time' and 'Remembrance of Things Past'. The book has been translated and the translations updated since by authors such as C K Scott Moncrieff, Terence Kilmartin, D J Enright and others, and now abridged by Zachary Whist.

Made in United States
North Haven, CT
16 November 2024

60411813R00178